Leiden

Travel Guide

Adventure

Discovering the Cultural Heart of the Netherlands.

by

Christopher Morrell

COPYRIGHT NOTICE

DISCLAIMER

Please note that the information contained within this document is for educational purposes only. The information contained herein has been obtained from sources believed to be reliable at the time of publication. The opinions expressed herein are subject to change without notice.

Readers acknowledge that the Author / Publisher is not engaging in rendering legal, financial or professional advice. The Publisher / Author disclaims all warranties as to the accuracy, completeness, or adequacy of such information.

The Publisher assumes no liability for errors, omissions, or inadequacies in the information contained herein or from the interpretations thereof. The publisher / Author specifically disclaims any liability from the use or application of the information contained herein or from the interpretations thereof.

TABLE OF CONTENT

Welcome to Leiden

Nestled between Amsterdam and The Hague, Leiden is a picturesque city that embodies the rich cultural heritage and vibrant academic life of the Netherlands. Known for its historic canals, stunning architecture, and deep intellectual history, Leiden offers a unique blend of old-world charm and modern innovation. Whether you are a first-time visitor eager to explore its cobbled streets or a returning admirer ready to delve deeper into its cultural offerings, this guidebook is your essential companion to experiencing the very best of Leiden.

As you traverse the city, you will encounter a captivating mix of classic Dutch landscapes and cutting-edge cultural sites. Leiden is not just a city; it's a journey through centuries of history, art, and science. Here, every alley and corner tells a story, from the legacy of the Pilgrims who stayed here before sailing to America, to the world-changing discoveries made by its university scholars.

In the pages that follow, we will guide you through Leiden's top attractions, hidden gems, and local favorites. With comprehensive itineraries, practical tips, and insights into the city's lifestyle, this guidebook is designed to ensure a memorable, enjoyable, and enriching visit. So let us begin our journey through Leiden, and discover why this city remains a treasure on the Dutch landscape.

Brief History

Founded in the 11th century, Leiden quickly rose to prominence in the Middle Ages as a major textile center, thanks to its strategic location on the Old Rhine river. The city's golden age came in the 16th and 17th centuries when it became a refuge for religious dissenters and intellectuals from across Europe, fostering a culture of tolerance and learning. This period also saw the founding of Leiden University in 1575, the oldest university in the Netherlands, which has since been at the forefront of scientific research and education.

Leiden's rich history is marred by the siege of 1574 during the Eighty Years' War, after which it quickly rebounded, becoming a center for printing and the arts. Renowned figures such as the painter Rembrandt and the scientist Herman Boerhaave called Leiden home, leaving an indelible mark on its cultural and intellectual life.

Overview of Leiden

Today, Leiden is celebrated for its beautiful canals, historic buildings, and vibrant university community. The city center, with its traditional Dutch architecture and the old fort known as the Burcht van Leiden, offers a glimpse into the past, while the numerous museums and galleries, like the Rijksmuseum van Oudheden and the Leiden American Pilgrim Museum, showcase its rich heritage.

Leiden's academic spirit is palpable in its bustling cafés and lively cultural scene, with festivals and events taking place throughout the year. The city's botanical gardens, the Hortus Botanicus, provide a peaceful retreat from the urban hustle, while the nearby North Sea beaches offer a refreshing escape.

Why Visit Leiden?

Leiden offers a unique blend of cultural depth, historical richness, and access to serene natural landscapes, including some of the Netherlands' most attractive beaches. Here's why you should consider Leiden for your next travel destination:

1. Cultural and Academic Hub: Explore the prestigious Leiden University, museums, and libraries that make the city a center for learning and culture.

2. Historical Heritage: Discover ancient buildings, beautiful churches, and winding canals that tell tales of the city's past as a major textile and trade center.

3. Artistic Legacy: Walk the streets that inspired Rembrandt and visit galleries that continue to celebrate his work and the work of contemporary artists.

4. Gateway to Dutch Beaches: Just a short journey from the city, the beaches of Katwijk and Noordwijk offer beautiful escapes with fine sands and rolling dunes—perfect for a day of relaxation or a quick seaside adventure.

5. Botanical Beauty: Enjoy the tranquility of the Hortus Botanicus, one of the oldest botanical gardens in the world, right in the heart of the city.

6. Festivals and Events: Participate in the vibrant local and international festivals that fill the city with music, art, and food all year round.

7. Culinary Delights: Indulge in a rich gastronomic scene from cozy cafés serving traditional Dutch snacks to fine dining establishments offering international cuisine.

8. Shopping and Leisure: Experience the eclectic shopping opportunities, from boutique fashion to antique books, all within the city's charming historical center.

9. Community Warmth: Engage with friendly locals who bring the city to life with their openness and hospitable nature, always ready to share a story or give a recommendation.

With all these exceptional features, it's clear why Leiden is a cherished destination for visitors globally. This guidebook is crafted to escort you through every facet of the city, supplying detailed information and expert recommendations to maximize your visit.

In the forthcoming chapters, you'll discover all the essentials needed to orchestrate your journey, from practical tips on navigating the city and selecting the ideal accommodations to comprehensive explorations of Leiden's principal attractions and lesser-known delights. We've also designed itineraries tailored to diverse types of travelers, whether you're in town for a brief weekend escape, a deep cultural immersion, an outdoor adventure, a trip with the family, or a vacation that's easy on the wallet.

Leiden is a city that truly offers something for everyone. We're thrilled to assist you in uncovering all its treasures. Let's embark on this fascinating exploration together. Turn the page and brace yourself to delve into the beauty, history, and vibrancy awaiting you in Leiden. Welcome to Leiden— where your adventure begins!

Chapter 1

How to Get to Leiden

Leiden is a gem nestled in the heart of the Netherlands, a city brimming with history, culture, and picturesque canals. As someone who has had the pleasure of exploring this charming city, I can assure you that getting to Leiden is quite straightforward, thanks to its excellent connectivity with major Dutch cities and international hubs. Here's a comprehensive guide on how you can reach Leiden by various modes of transportation.

By Air

Flying into the Netherlands is the quickest way to start your adventure in Leiden. The nearest major airport is Amsterdam Schiphol Airport (AMS), which is one of the busiest airports in Europe. From almost anywhere in the world, you can find a direct flight to Schiphol. Once you land, getting to Leiden is a breeze.

Schiphol Airport is about 25 kilometers from Leiden, and there are several convenient ways to travel from the airport to the city. The most efficient option is to take a train. The Nederlandse Spoorwegen (NS) train service operates direct trains from Schiphol Airport to Leiden Central Station. The trains run frequently, approximately every 15 minutes, and the journey takes just around 20 minutes. Tickets can be purchased at the airport's train station, either from ticket machines or the NS service desk. A one-way ticket costs about €6.

During my trip, I found the train service to be incredibly efficient and comfortable. The trains are modern, clean, and equipped with free Wi-Fi, making the short journey quite pleasant. Plus, the views of the

Dutch countryside are a lovely introduction to the beauty of the Netherlands.

If you prefer a more private transfer, taxis are readily available at Schiphol Airport. A taxi ride to Leiden takes about 30 minutes and costs approximately €50-€70, depending on traffic. I took a taxi once when I had heavy luggage, and it was convenient and hassle-free. For pre-booking, you can contact Schiphol Taxi at +31 20 653 1000.

By Train

For those already in Europe, traveling to Leiden by train is an excellent option. The Netherlands has an extensive and efficient rail network, and Leiden is well-connected to major Dutch cities like Amsterdam, The Hague, Rotterdam, and Utrecht.

If you're coming from Amsterdam, you can catch a direct train to Leiden Central Station. The journey takes about 35 minutes, and trains run every 10-15 minutes. A standard one-way ticket costs around

€10.50. The train ride offers a scenic view of the Dutch landscape, with its iconic windmills and lush green fields.

Traveling from The Hague is even quicker. The train ride from Den Haag Centraal to Leiden Central Station takes just 12 minutes, with tickets priced at around €5 for a one-way trip. The convenience of frequent trains makes it easy to plan your travel without worrying about long waits.

From Rotterdam, the train journey to Leiden takes about 35 minutes, with tickets costing approximately €11 for a one-way trip. Utrecht to Leiden is a bit longer, around 45 minutes, and a one-way ticket costs around €12.50. Regardless of where you're coming from, the trains are punctual, comfortable, and offer a relaxing way to travel.

One memorable trip I had was taking an early morning train from Amsterdam. The serene countryside, bathed in the soft morning light, was a sight to behold. The journey was so smooth that I almost didn't want it to end!

By Bus

While trains are generally the preferred mode of transport, buses are also a viable option for getting to Leiden. FlixBus and other long-distance bus services operate routes that connect Leiden with several European cities. This can be a cost-effective option, especially for budget travelers.

From Amsterdam, you can take a FlixBus to Leiden. The journey takes about an hour, and tickets can be as cheap as €5 if booked in advance. The bus stops at Leiden Central Station, making it convenient to transfer to other parts of the city.

For those traveling from The Hague, the bus ride to Leiden is about 30 minutes, with tickets priced around €4. Buses from Rotterdam to Leiden take about 45 minutes, with tickets costing approximately €6.50.

From Utrecht, the bus journey takes about an hour, and tickets are usually around €8.

On one of my trips, I opted for a FlixBus from Brussels to Leiden. It was a long journey, about three hours, but the bus was comfortable, and the price was unbeatable. Plus, it gave me a chance to catch up on some reading while watching the European countryside roll by.

By Car

Driving to Leiden is another option, especially if you enjoy the freedom of exploring at your own pace. The Netherlands has an excellent road network, and driving can be a pleasant experience. If you're arriving from Schiphol Airport, renting a car is straightforward. Major car rental companies like Hertz, Avis, and Europcar have desks at the airport.

The drive from Schiphol Airport to Leiden takes about 30 minutes via the A4 motorway. The roads are well-marked, and GPS navigation makes it easy to find your way. Just be mindful of the Dutch traffic rules and speed limits, which are strictly enforced.

If you're coming from Amsterdam, the drive to Leiden is about 45 minutes, depending on traffic. From The Hague, it's a quick 25-minute drive via the A44 motorway. Driving from Rotterdam to Leiden takes about 45 minutes, while the journey from Utrecht is around an hour.

One of the advantages of driving is the ability to stop and explore along the way. On one of my drives to Leiden, I took a detour to visit the Keukenhof Gardens, famous for its stunning tulip displays. It was a delightful break in the journey and one of the highlights of my trip.

Parking in Leiden can be a bit challenging, especially in the city center. However, there are several parking garages where you can safely leave your car. Parking garage Morspoort, located at Morssingel 2, 2312 AZ Leiden, is a convenient option, and their phone number is +31 71 514 0711. Another good choice is the

Parking Garage Lammermarkt at Lammermarkt 10, 2312 CW Leiden, with a contact number of +31 71 514 4983. Parking fees typically range from €2 to €4 per hour.

Personal Reflections

My journeys to Leiden have always been smooth and enjoyable, regardless of the mode of transportation. Each option has its own charm and convenience, catering to different preferences and travel styles.

Flying into Schiphol and taking the train is my top recommendation for international travelers. It's quick, efficient, and offers a seamless transition from the plane to the heart of Leiden. The Dutch rail system is something to be admired for its punctuality and comfort.

For those already in Europe, traveling by train is a wonderful way to see more of the Netherlands. The scenic routes and the convenience of frequent services make it an ideal choice. Buses are a great budget option, especially if you don't mind a longer journey and want to save some euros.

Driving gives you the freedom to explore at your own pace and discover hidden gems along the way. Just be prepared for parking challenges in the city center and always follow local traffic regulations.

Whichever way you choose to arrive in Leiden, the city's charm and warmth will welcome you with open arms. The journey is just the beginning of an unforgettable adventure in this beautiful Dutch city.

In conclusion, getting to Leiden is easy and accessible, whether you're flying in from afar, taking a scenic train ride, hopping on a budget-friendly bus, or enjoying a road trip. The city's well-connected transport links ensure that your journey is smooth and enjoyable. Once you arrive, you'll be ready to explore the rich history, vibrant culture, and stunning beauty that Leiden has to offer. Happy travels, and I hope you enjoy your time in this enchanting city as much as I did!

Chapter 2

How to Get Around Leiden

Navigating Leiden, with its charming canals, historic architecture, and vibrant atmosphere, is a delightful experience. During my time in this enchanting city, I discovered various modes of transportation that made exploring both convenient and enjoyable. Here's a comprehensive guide to help you get around Leiden like a local.

Public Transportation

Leiden's public transportation system is efficient and well-connected, making it easy to travel within the city and to nearby areas. The bus network, operated by Arriva, is the backbone of public transport in Leiden. The central hub for buses is the Leiden Centraal Station, located at Stationsplein 1, 2312 AJ Leiden. You can contact the station at +31 900 9292.

The buses are reliable, clean, and frequent, with routes covering all major areas of the city. A single ticket costs around €2.50, but if you plan to use the bus multiple times, I recommend getting an OV-chipkaart. This rechargeable card can be used on all public transport in the Netherlands and offers discounted fares. You can purchase an OV-chipkaart at the train station or various convenience stores like Albert Heijn or Kruidvat. Using this card, a typical bus ride costs around €1.50 to €2, depending on the distance traveled.

For longer distances or trips to neighboring cities, the train is an excellent option. Leiden Centraal Station is a major railway hub, with frequent trains to Amsterdam, Rotterdam, The Hague, and other cities. A one-way ticket to Amsterdam costs approximately €10.40 and takes about 35 minutes. The trains are modern, comfortable, and offer free Wi-Fi, which is perfect for catching up on emails or planning your next destination.

Car Rentals

While public transport is excellent, renting a car can provide flexibility, especially if you plan to explore the surrounding countryside or visit smaller towns. Several car rental companies operate in Leiden, offering a range of vehicles to suit your needs.

During my stay, I rented a car from Hertz, located at Bargelaan 8, 2333 CT Leiden, near the train station. Their contact number is +31 71 514 0496. The process was straightforward, and the staff was friendly and helpful. Prices vary depending on the type of car and rental duration, but you can expect to pay around €40 to €70 per day for a standard vehicle.

Driving in Leiden is relatively easy, but it's essential to be aware of the many cyclists and pedestrians. Parking can be challenging in the city center, especially during peak hours. However, there are several parking garages and park-and-ride facilities on the outskirts of the city, which are more convenient and often cheaper. The Morspoort parking garage, located at Langegracht 38, 2312 NW Leiden, charges about €2.50 per hour or €12.50 for a full day.

Biking and Walking

One of the most enjoyable ways to explore Leiden is by bike. The city is incredibly bike-friendly, with dedicated bike lanes and plenty of bike rental shops. Cycling allows you to see the city at your own pace, discover hidden gems, and enjoy the scenic routes along the canals and parks.

I rented my bike from EasyFiets, located at Breestraat 65, 2311 CJ Leiden. Their phone number is +31 71 512 3111. They offer a range of bikes, including traditional Dutch bikes and electric bikes, with prices starting at €8 per day for a standard bike. Renting a bike for a week is more economical, costing around €35. The staff provided a map of the best cycling routes and some great local tips.

Leiden's compact size makes it perfect for walking as well. Strolling through the city allows you to appreciate the beautiful architecture, quaint streets, and vibrant atmosphere. Some of my favorite walks included wandering through the botanical gardens at Hortus Botanicus, located at Rapenburg 73, 2311 GJ Leiden, and exploring the historic Pieterskwartier district with its charming houses and narrow alleys.

Tips for Navigating the City

Plan Your Routes: Whether you're walking, biking, or using public transport, planning your routes can save time and help you make the most of your visit. I used the 9292 app for public transport, which provides real-time information and route planning. For biking and walking, Google Maps and the local maps provided by rental shops were invaluable.

Stay Safe: If you're biking, always follow the local traffic rules. Use bike lanes where available, signal your turns, and be mindful of pedestrians. At night, make sure your bike lights are working, as it's required by law.

Be Aware of Pedestrian Zones: The city center has several pedestrian-only areas, especially around shopping streets like Haarlemmerstraat. These zones are perfect for leisurely walks without the worry of traffic.

Embrace the Canal Culture: Leiden's canals are a significant part of the city's charm. Consider renting a boat or joining a canal tour to see the city from a different perspective. Companies like Bootjes en Broodjes, located at Blauwpoortshaven 5, 2312 EL Leiden, offer boat rentals starting at €25 per hour. Their contact number is +31 71 513 2113.

Local Etiquette: The Dutch are known for their directness and friendliness. When asking for directions or help, don't hesitate to approach locals—they're usually very willing to assist. Basic Dutch phrases like "Dank u wel" (Thank you) and "Alstublieft" (Please) are appreciated and show respect for the local culture.

Use a Travel Card: If you're staying for an extended period, consider getting a Leiden Pass, which offers discounts on transport, attractions, and dining. It's available at the VVV Leiden Tourist Information Center, located at Stationsweg 26, 2312 AV Leiden. Their phone number is +31 71 516 6000.

Leiden's charm lies in its accessibility and the ease with which you can explore its many wonders. Whether you're zipping through the streets on a bike, meandering along the canals on foot, or hopping on a bus or train, each mode of transport offers a unique perspective of this beautiful city. My time in Leiden was filled with delightful discoveries, and I hope these tips help you navigate the city with confidence and joy. Happy exploring!

IMPORTANT INFORMATION:

"Please kindly use Google Maps on your phone to get recent pictures and real-time directions from your current location to your destination by simply inputting the addresses found in this book. Thank you."

Chapter 3

Top Tourist Attractions in Leiden, Netherlands

Discover Historic Sites

The Netherlands' Oldest University: Leiden University

One of my first stops in Leiden was the iconic Leiden University, the oldest university in the Netherlands, founded in 1575. Walking through the campus, I could almost feel the weight of history in the air. The old buildings, with their classic Dutch architecture, are steeped in stories of scholars and students who have walked these paths for centuries.

Address: Rapenburg 70, 2311 EZ Leiden

Phone: +31 71 527 2727

I spent an afternoon exploring the Academy Building, the heart of the university. The interior is adorned with portraits of past professors, adding a sense of gravitas. The Hortus Botanicus, the university's botanical garden, was another highlight. Established in 1590, it's one of the oldest botanical gardens in the world. The entry fee is €7.50, but it's worth every penny for the serene beauty and the variety of plant species, some of which are quite rare.

Personal Tip: If you visit in the spring, you'll be treated to the sight of blooming tulips, a quintessentially Dutch experience.

Pieterskerk: A Medieval Masterpiece

Another must-visit historic site is Pieterskerk, a Gothic church that dates back to 1121. As I walked into the grand hall, I was awestruck by the towering columns and the beautiful stained glass windows. The church's interior is both majestic and peaceful, offering a quiet respite from the bustling city outside.

Address: Pieterskerkhof 1a, 2311 SP Leiden

Phone: +31 71 512 4140

Entry Fee: €5

I learned that this church is the final resting place of several notable figures, including the painter Jan Steen and the Pilgrim Fathers, who later sailed to America on the Mayflower. The church often hosts concerts and exhibitions, so it's worth checking their schedule in advance.

Personal Experience: During my visit, there was a beautiful organ concert that filled the church with heavenly music. It was a truly magical experience.

Leiden American Pilgrim Museum

Tucked away in a quaint old house is the Leiden American Pilgrim Museum, which provides a fascinating glimpse into the lives of the Pilgrims before they left for the New World. The museum is small but rich in history, with artifacts dating back to the early 17th century.

Address: Beschuitsteeg 9, 2312 JT Leiden

Phone: +31 71 512 2413

Entry Fee: €9

The knowledgeable staff shared intriguing stories and detailed explanations about the exhibits. It's a must-visit for history buffs and anyone interested in the Pilgrim Fathers' story.

Personal Tip: The museum is only open from Wednesday to Saturday, so plan your visit accordingly.

Explore Scenic Parks

Hortus Botanicus: A Green Oasis

While technically part of the university, the Hortus Botanicus deserves its own mention as a top attraction. The gardens are divided into several sections, including a tropical greenhouse, a winter garden, and a large outdoor area with ponds and winding paths.

Address: Rapenburg 73, 2311 GJ Leiden

Phone: +31 71 527 7249

Entry Fee: €7.50

I spent hours wandering through the gardens, taking in the sights and smells of countless plant species. The Clusiustuin, a reconstructed 16th-century garden, was particularly charming.

Personal Experience: There's a cozy café in the garden where I enjoyed a cup of Dutch coffee and a slice of apple pie while soaking in the tranquil surroundings.

Plantsoen Park: A Perfect Spot for Relaxation

Plantsoen Park, located in the heart of Leiden, is a lovely place to relax and unwind. The park features winding paths, picturesque bridges, and plenty of benches where you can sit and watch the world go by.

Address: Plantsoen, 2311 Leiden

During my visit, I saw locals jogging, walking their dogs, and having picnics. The park is especially beautiful in the autumn when the leaves turn vibrant shades of red and orange.

Personal Tip: Bring a blanket and some snacks for a leisurely picnic by the pond.

Leiden's Canals: A Scenic Stroll

Leiden's canals are an integral part of the city's charm. I loved walking along the water's edge, crossing the quaint bridges, and watching the boats glide by. The reflections of the historic buildings in the water create a picturesque scene that feels straight out of a painting.

Starting Point: Beestenmarkt, 2312 CC Leiden

I highly recommend taking a canal tour to see the city from a different perspective. The boat tours usually cost around €12 per person and last about an hour. It's a relaxing way to learn more about Leiden's history and architecture.

Personal Experience: I took a sunset canal tour, and the golden light on the buildings made for some stunning photographs.

Visit Iconic Landmarks

The Burcht: A Medieval Fortification

One of the most iconic landmarks in Leiden is The Burcht, an ancient fortress perched on a small hill in the city center. The climb to the top is steep, but the panoramic views of Leiden from the summit are absolutely worth it.

Address: Burgsteeg 14, 2312 JS Leiden

Entry Fee: Free

The Burcht dates back to the 9th century and has been beautifully preserved. Walking around the circular walls, I imagined what it must have been like to defend the city from this vantage point.

Personal Tip: Visit early in the morning to avoid the crowds and enjoy a peaceful moment overlooking the city.

National Museum of Antiquities

For anyone interested in ancient history, the National Museum of Antiquities (Rijksmuseum van Oudheden) is a treasure trove of artifacts from ancient Egypt, Greece, and Rome. The museum's collection is impressive, with everything from mummies to classical sculptures.

Address: Rapenburg 28, 2311 EW Leiden

Phone: +31 71 516 3163

Entry Fee: €12.50

I was particularly fascinated by the Egyptian gallery, which houses an authentic temple transported from Egypt. The museum is well laid out, with detailed information in both Dutch and English.

Personal Experience: The interactive exhibits and the well-curated displays kept me engaged for hours. It's a great place to spend a rainy afternoon.

Molen de Valk: The Falcon Windmill

No visit to the Netherlands would be complete without seeing a traditional windmill, and Molen de Valk (The Falcon) is a perfect example. This windmill, which dates back to 1743, has been converted into a museum that showcases the history of milling.

Address: 2e Binnenvestgracht 1, 2312 BZ Leiden

Phone: +31 71 516 5353

Entry Fee: €5

Climbing up the windmill's interior, I gained insight into the lives of the millers and the workings of the mill. The views from the top are fantastic, offering another great vantage point over Leiden.

Personal Tip: Be sure to visit the gift shop for some unique windmill-themed souvenirs.

Museum Volkenkunde: A World of Cultures

While not as famous as some of the other museums, Museum Volkenkunde is a hidden gem that shouldn't be missed. This museum is dedicated to the cultures of the world, with exhibits from Asia, Africa, Oceania, and the Americas.

Address: Steenstraat 1, 2312 BS Leiden

Phone: +31 71 516 8800

Entry Fee: €14

The museum's layout is engaging, with interactive displays and artifacts that bring global cultures to life. I was particularly drawn to the Japanese and Polynesian sections, which feature beautiful art and intriguing objects.

Personal Experience: The museum often hosts temporary exhibitions and cultural events, so check the schedule before you go. I was lucky enough to catch a traditional Japanese tea ceremony demonstration.

Leidse Hout: A Tranquil Retreat

Leidse Hout is a beautiful park that feels like a hidden oasis. Located a bit off the beaten path, it's a perfect place for a quiet walk, a jog, or just to relax in nature.

Address: Houtlaan 100, 2334 CL Leiden

The park features lovely wooded areas, open meadows, and a charming pond. There's also a small petting zoo that's great for families with children.

Personal Tip: Pack a picnic and enjoy a leisurely afternoon under the trees. The park is especially lovely in the spring when the flowers are in bloom.

SieboldHuis: Japan in Leiden

One of the more unique attractions in Leiden is the SieboldHuis, a museum dedicated to Japanese art and culture. The museum is housed in a beautiful historic building and offers a fascinating glimpse into the life of Philipp Franz von Siebold, a German doctor who lived in Japan during the 19th century.

Address: Rapenburg 19, 2311 GE Leiden

Phone: +31 71 512 5539

Entry Fee: €8.50

The exhibits include a range of Japanese artifacts, from samurai armor to delicate ceramics. The museum also has beautiful Japanese gardens that are perfect for a peaceful stroll.

Personal Experience: The guided tour was incredibly informative, and I learned a lot about the cultural exchange between Japan and the Netherlands.

De Zijlpoort: A Historical Gateway

De Zijlpoort is one of the remaining city gates of Leiden and a beautiful piece of historical architecture. Built in 1667, this gate once served as a main entrance to the city and is now a picturesque landmark.

Address: Zijlpoort, Zijlvest 41, 2312 MV Leiden

Walking through the gate, I felt a deep connection to the city's past. The surrounding area is also lovely, with scenic views along the canal.

Personal Tip: Stop by the nearby café for a drink and enjoy the view of the gate and canal. It's a great spot for some quiet reflection.

Conclusion

Leiden is a city that truly captures the heart with its rich history, beautiful parks, iconic landmarks, and hidden gems. Each corner of this charming city has a story to tell, and spending time here has given me a deep appreciation for its cultural and historical significance. Whether you're wandering through ancient university halls, relaxing in a tranquil park, or uncovering the secrets of its hidden gems, Leiden promises an unforgettable journey. So pack your bags, bring your curiosity, and get ready to explore the wonders of Leiden, Netherlands. Safe travels!

Chapter 4

Beaches Near Leiden

Nestled in the heart of the Netherlands, Leiden is a city teeming with history, culture, and vibrant student life. But beyond the charming canals and centuries-old architecture, there's another side to explore — the stunning Dutch coastline. Just a short trip from Leiden, you'll find a variety of beautiful beaches that offer everything from peaceful relaxation to exhilarating water sports. Having spent several sun-soaked days exploring these coastal gems, I'm thrilled to share my personal experiences and tips to help you make the most of your beach adventures near Leiden.

Overview of Nearby Beaches

The Dutch coastline is a treasure trove of sandy stretches and scenic views, and the beaches near Leiden are no exception. The North Sea's crisp, bracing waters, combined with the soft, golden sands, make for an unforgettable seaside experience. Here are some of the beaches you absolutely must visit:

Katwijk aan Zee: A family-friendly beach with a quaint village atmosphere.

Noordwijk: Known for its lively promenade and water sports.

Scheveningen: A bustling resort town with plenty of entertainment options.

Wassenaar: A serene escape perfect for those seeking tranquility.

Each of these beaches has its unique charm and appeal, so let's dive into the details.

Best Beaches for Relaxation

Katwijk aan Zee: Tranquil and Picturesque

Katwijk aan Zee is my go-to beach when I need to unwind and escape the hustle and bustle of daily life. This charming seaside village is just a 20-minute drive from Leiden, making it incredibly accessible. The beach itself is clean and well-maintained, with plenty of space to lay down a towel and soak up the sun.

Address: Boulevard Zeezijde 39, 2225 BB Katwijk aan Zee

Personal Experience: On my first visit, I spent the afternoon strolling along the sandy shore, collecting seashells and enjoying the gentle sea breeze. I particularly loved the peaceful ambiance, which is perfect for reading a book or simply relaxing with the sound of waves in the background. For a delicious lunch, I highly recommend Het Strand, a beachfront restaurant where you can enjoy fresh seafood dishes. The shrimp croquettes (€12) were a highlight!

Wassenaar Beach: Serenity by the Sea

If you're looking for a quieter spot to relax, Wassenaar Beach is an excellent choice. This lesser-known gem is a bit further from Leiden but well worth the trip. The beach is surrounded by dunes and offers a more secluded and natural environment compared to the busier beaches.

Address: Wassenaarseslag 26, 2242 PJ Wassenaar

Personal Tip: I often visit this beach early in the morning when it's practically deserted. There's something incredibly calming about watching the sunrise over the North Sea. Don't forget to bring a picnic – there's nothing quite like enjoying a homemade meal while taking in the breathtaking coastal views. For those interested in a bit of exploration, the nearby Meijendel Nature Reserve offers beautiful hiking trails through the dunes.

Top Spots for Water Activities

Noordwijk: Adventure and Excitement

For those who crave a bit more action, Noordwijk is the beach to visit. Known as the "beach of Amsterdam," it's popular among locals and tourists alike for its wide range of water sports. Whether you're into surfing, kiteboarding, or windsurfing, Noordwijk has it all.

Address: Koningin Astrid Boulevard 5, 2202 BK Noordwijk

Personal Experience: My friends and I decided to try our hand at windsurfing, and we had an absolute blast. We took a beginner's lesson at the local surf school, which cost around €50 per person for a two-hour session. The instructors were patient and knowledgeable, making the experience both fun and educational. Afterward, we relaxed at Beachclub O, enjoying some refreshing cocktails (around €10 each) while watching the more experienced surfers ride the waves.

Scheveningen: The Ultimate Beach Resort

Scheveningen is arguably the most famous beach in the Netherlands, and for good reason. This lively resort town offers a plethora of activities both on and off the water. From paddleboarding to jet skiing, there's no shortage of ways to get your adrenaline pumping.

Address: Strandweg 9, 2586 JK The Hague

Personal Tip: One of the highlights of my visit to Scheveningen was taking a ride on the giant Ferris wheel on the pier. The views from the top are absolutely stunning, offering a panoramic vista of the beach and beyond. Tickets are reasonably priced at €9 for adults and €6 for children. After a day of water activities, I recommend grabbing dinner at Simonis Aan Zee. Their seafood platter (€35) is to die for and perfect for sharing.

Hidden Coastal Treasures

Zandvoort: A Blend of Nature and Nightlife

Zandvoort is a bit of a hidden gem, offering a unique blend of natural beauty and vibrant nightlife. This beach is located slightly further north of Noordwijk and is easily accessible by train from Leiden. The town itself has a charming vibe, with plenty of bars and restaurants to explore.

Address: Boulevard Barnaart 23, 2041 JA Zandvoort

Personal Experience: One evening, I stumbled upon Ubuntu Beach, a cozy beach bar with a relaxed, bohemian atmosphere. It's the perfect place to watch the sunset with a glass of wine (€6). The town also has a casino if you're feeling lucky. For a bit of adventure, I took a walk through the nearby Zuid-Kennemerland National Park, where you can spot wild deer and enjoy the scenic dune landscapes.

Langevelderslag: Off the Beaten Path

For those who prefer to venture off the beaten path, Langevelderslag is an excellent choice. This beach is tucked away between Noordwijk and Zandvoort and is less frequented by tourists. The area is known for its stunning dune landscapes and peaceful environment.

Address: Langevelderslag 2, 2204 AH Noordwijkerhout

Personal Tip: This is a great spot for a quiet day trip. I brought my bike and cycled along the scenic routes through the dunes, stopping occasionally to take in the views. There are also several walking trails for those who prefer to explore on foot. Pack a picnic and plenty of water, as there aren't many facilities nearby. For a sweet treat, stop by Strandpaviljoen Nederzandt. Their apple pie (€5) is a must-try!

Conclusion

The beaches near Leiden offer a diverse array of experiences, from the bustling activity of Noordwijk and Scheveningen to the serene, hidden gems of Wassenaar and Langevelderslag. Whether you're looking to relax, engage in thrilling water sports, or discover lesser-known coastal treasures, there's something for everyone.

Each of these beaches has left a lasting impression on me, and I hope my personal experiences and tips help you make the most of your own adventures. So, pack your sunscreen, grab your beach towel, and get ready to explore the stunning coastline near Leiden. Happy beach-hopping!

Chapter 5

How to Experience Leiden's Culture

Leiden, a gem in the Netherlands, is a city brimming with culture, history, and charm. As someone who has wandered through its picturesque streets and interacted with its warm-hearted locals, I can say that Leiden's cultural scene is a treasure trove waiting to be discovered. Whether you're a history buff, a food lover, or a music enthusiast, Leiden offers something for everyone. Let me take you through some of the highlights of experiencing Leiden's culture, from its world-class museums and vibrant festivals to its delectable cuisine and enchanting traditional music.

Museums and Galleries

Leiden is home to some of the most remarkable museums and galleries in the Netherlands, making it a haven for art and history enthusiasts. One of my favorite places is the Rijksmuseum van Oudheden

(National Museum of Antiquities). Located at Rapenburg 28, 2311 EW Leiden, this museum is a treasure trove of ancient artifacts from Egypt, Greece, and Rome. Walking through the halls adorned with mummies, statues, and ancient tools, I felt like I was traveling back in time. The entry fee is €12.50 for adults, and it's worth every penny. You can contact them at +31 71 516 3163 for more information.

Another must-visit is the Museum De Lakenhal, located at Oude Singel 32, 2312 RA Leiden. This museum beautifully captures Leiden's rich history and its pivotal role in the Dutch Golden Age. The art collection here is impressive, with works from famous Dutch masters like Rembrandt, who was born in Leiden. I spent hours admiring the paintings and learning about the city's textile industry, which was fascinating. The entrance fee is €10 for adults. For inquiries, you can reach them at +31 71 516 5360.

For those interested in natural history, the Naturalis Biodiversity Center is a must-see. Situated at Darwinweg 2, 2333 CR Leiden, this museum is a delightful blend of education and entertainment. The dinosaur skeletons are a hit with both kids and adults. I particularly enjoyed the interactive exhibits that make learning about biodiversity fun and engaging. Tickets are priced at €14 for adults. Their contact number is +31 71 751 9519.

Festivals and Events

Leiden is a city that knows how to celebrate, and its festivals and events are a testament to its vibrant culture. One of the most exciting events is the Leiden International Film Festival (LIFF), which takes place every November. As a movie buff, I was thrilled to attend screenings of independent films from around the world. The festival atmosphere is lively, with plenty of opportunities to meet filmmakers and fellow cinema enthusiasts. The main venue is Trianon Theater, located at Breestraat 31, 2311 CH Leiden. You can contact them at +31 71 512 2901.

Another highlight of my time in Leiden was the Leidens Ontzet (Relief of Leiden), celebrated every October 3rd. This historical festival commemorates the end of the Spanish siege in 1574. The entire city comes alive with parades, music, food stalls, and funfair rides. I joined the locals in eating hutspot (a traditional stew) and herring, which are traditional dishes for this event. The sense of community and the joyous atmosphere make this a must-experience event if you're in Leiden in early October.

For music lovers, the Leiden Jazz Week held in January is a fantastic event. Various venues across the city host performances by both local and international jazz artists. I remember spending an evening at Jazz Café The Duke, located at Noordeinde 39, 2311 CA Leiden, grooving to some fantastic live jazz. The entry fees vary by event, but you can contact The Duke at +31 71 514 9956 for more details.

Local Cuisine and Dining

Exploring Leiden's culinary scene was one of the most delightful parts of my visit. The city offers a plethora of dining options, from cozy cafés to upscale restaurants, each serving delicious dishes that reflect the region's rich culinary heritage.

One of my favorite spots for a hearty meal was Oudt Leyden, located at Steenstraat 49, 2312 BV Leiden. This restaurant is famous for its traditional Dutch pancakes, and I couldn't resist trying the apple and bacon variety. It was a perfect blend of sweet and savory, and the cozy atmosphere made it even better. A meal here costs around €15-€20 per person. You can reserve a table by calling +31 71 513 3144.

For a taste of contemporary Dutch cuisine, I highly recommend Het Prentenkabinet. Nestled in a historic building at Kloksteeg 25, 2311 SK Leiden, this restaurant offers a delightful dining experience. I enjoyed their seasonal tasting menu, which featured fresh, locally sourced ingredients. The wine pairings were superb and complemented the dishes perfectly. Dining here is a bit pricier, with meals costing around €40-€60 per person, but it's worth the splurge. Their phone number is +31 71 512 6666.

If you're in the mood for something more casual, Café Barrera at Rapenburg 56, 2311 GH Leiden, is a great choice. This charming café is perfect for a relaxed lunch or a coffee break. I loved their selection of sandwiches and pastries, and the outdoor seating area offers a lovely view of the canal. Prices are reasonable, with most items costing between €5-€15. You can reach them at +31 71 514 4477.

Traditional Music and Dance

Music and dance are integral parts of Leiden's cultural fabric, and experiencing them firsthand was truly magical. The city has a rich tradition of folk music, and I was fortunate to catch a performance by a local folk band at Burcht van Leiden, an ancient fortification turned public park. The lively tunes and the audience's enthusiasm made it an unforgettable evening. The park is located at Burgsteeg 14, 2312 JS Leiden, and while the performances are usually free, it's a good idea to check local listings for scheduled events.

For those interested in classical music, the Stadsgehoorzaal Leiden is the place to be. This beautiful concert hall at Breestraat 60, 2311 CS Leiden, hosts performances by renowned orchestras and soloists. I attended a stunning concert by the Leiden Symphony Orchestra, and the acoustics were phenomenal. Ticket prices vary depending on the event, but you can expect to pay around €20-€50. For more information, call +31 71 516 2400.

Dance enthusiasts should not miss the Leiden Dance Theater, where contemporary dance performances showcase the incredible talent of both local and international dancers. I was captivated by a modern dance performance that combined innovative choreography with stunning visuals. The theater is located at Bargelaan 190, 2333 CW Leiden, and tickets usually range from €15-€40. You can contact them at +31 71 516 3881 for the latest schedule.

Leiden also hosts traditional Dutch dance events, where you can watch or even participate in folk dances. I joined a local dance group for a session at Volkstuinvereniging Ons Buiten, an allotment garden where community events are often held. The dance steps were simple and fun, and it was a fantastic way to connect with the locals. The garden is located at

Vinkweg 1, 2317 WK Leiden. You can call +31 71 572 1234 to find out about upcoming events.

Personal Reflections

Experiencing Leiden's culture was a journey filled with joy, learning, and connection. The city's museums and galleries provided a deep dive into its rich history and artistic heritage, while the festivals and events showcased the lively and communal spirit of the people. Dining in Leiden was a gastronomic adventure, offering everything from traditional dishes to modern culinary creations. And the music and dance performances added a beautiful rhythm to my days in this enchanting city.

One of my most memorable moments was during the Leidens Ontzet festival. As I stood among the crowd, watching the fireworks light up the sky over the historic city, I felt a profound sense of belonging. The stories shared by locals, the taste of hutspot, and the sounds of laughter and celebration created an atmosphere of warmth and camaraderie that I will never forget.

Leiden is a city that invites you to immerse yourself in its culture, to participate, to learn, and to celebrate. Whether you're visiting for the first time or returning for another adventure, there's always something new to discover. Embrace the opportunity to explore its museums, join in its festivals, savor its cuisine, and dance to its tunes. Let Leiden's culture enrich your journey and leave you with memories that will last a lifetime.

I hope this guide inspires you to experience Leiden's culture to the fullest. Safe travels, and enjoy every moment in this beautiful city!

Chapter 6

Outdoor Adventures in Leiden

L eiden, with its charming canals and historic architecture, might not be the first place you think of when it comes to outdoor adventures. But trust me, this quaint Dutch city has a lot to offer for those who love nature and the great outdoors. I spent several weeks exploring the green spaces, waterways, and natural reserves around Leiden, and I can't wait to share my experiences with you. Whether you enjoy hiking, bird watching, or water sports, Leiden has something for every outdoor enthusiast.

Hiking and Nature Trails

When I first arrived in Leiden, I was eager to find a peaceful place to walk and soak in the natural beauty of the area. One of the best spots for hiking is the Boterhuispolder, a serene nature reserve just a short bike ride from the city center. The trails here are well-marked and perfect for a leisurely stroll or a more vigorous hike. The fresh air and the sight of cows grazing in the meadows make it a truly Dutch experience. You can access the Boterhuispolder from the entrance near Merenwijk, and there's no entry fee, which makes it a great budget-friendly option.

For those who prefer a more structured hiking experience, the Leidse Hout park offers a variety of trails that wind through beautiful woodlands and past picturesque ponds. I loved spending afternoons here, especially in the spring when the flowers are in full bloom. The park is located at Houtlaan 100, 2334 CL Leiden, and the best part is that it's free to enter. There's also a lovely café in the park, where you can grab a coffee or a light lunch after your hike.

If you're looking for something a bit more challenging, head to the nearby dunes at Meijendel. This nature reserve offers an extensive network of trails that take you through sand dunes, forests, and along the coast. The views are breathtaking, and it's a great place to see some of the unique flora and fauna of the region. Meijendel is about a 30-minute drive from Leiden, and there's a small parking fee of around €2 per hour. The main entrance is located at Meijendelseweg 40, 2243 GN Wassenaar.

National and Natural Parks

One of my favorite excursions was a visit to the Nationaal Park Hollandse Duinen. This expansive park stretches along the coast and includes dunes, beaches, and woodlands. The diversity of landscapes here is incredible, and it's a fantastic place for hiking, biking, and even horseback riding. I spent an entire day exploring the various trails, and I still feel like I only scratched the surface. The park is open year-round, and entrance is free. The visitor center, where you can get maps and information, is located at Zeeweg 12, 2202 HA Noordwijk.

Another must-visit is the Zuid-Kennemerland National Park, which is slightly further afield but well worth the trip. This park offers a unique combination of dunes, forests, and open grasslands, and it's home to a variety of wildlife, including deer and foxes. I took a guided tour, which cost about €15, and it was fascinating to learn about the park's ecosystems and history. The main entrance is at Zeeweg 12, 2051 EC Overveen, and there's a small parking fee.

Closer to Leiden, the Kagerplassen is a series of lakes and canals that provide a wonderful setting for outdoor activities. This area is particularly popular for boating and sailing, but there are also lovely walking paths along the water. I rented a small sailboat for a few hours for around €50 and enjoyed a relaxing afternoon on the water. There are several rental companies in the area, including Kagerzoom at Julianalaan 1, 2159 LB Kaag.

Water Activities and Sports

Leiden's network of canals and nearby lakes make it an ideal destination for water sports. One of the most enjoyable activities I tried was kayaking through the city's canals. It's a unique way to see the historic buildings and bridges from a different perspective. You can rent kayaks from Bootjes en Broodjes, located at Blauwpoortsbrug 1, 2312 GA Leiden. They offer hourly rentals starting at €10, and they also provide guided tours if you prefer a more structured experience.

For a more adventurous water activity, I highly recommend windsurfing or kitesurfing at the nearby beaches. I took a beginner's windsurfing lesson at the Surf School Noordwijk, which is about a 20-minute drive from Leiden. The instructors were fantastic, and I had so much fun learning to ride the waves. Lessons start at around €50 for a two-hour session, and you can find the school at Koningin Astrid Boulevard 106, 2202 BD Noordwijk.

If you're interested in sailing, the Vlietlanden area is perfect for both beginners and experienced sailors. I joined a sailing trip organized by a local club, which was a great way to meet other enthusiasts and enjoy the beautiful scenery. The sailing club, Watersportvereniging Vlietland, is located at Vlietweg 128, 2266 LB Leidschendam, and they offer various courses and rental options.

Bird Watching

Bird watching is a popular activity in and around Leiden, thanks to the region's diverse habitats and abundance of bird species. One of the best places for bird watching is the Groene Hart, a vast green area that surrounds Leiden. I spent several mornings there with my binoculars, spotting a variety of birds, including herons, storks, and numerous songbirds. The area is crisscrossed with walking and biking trails, making it easy to explore.

Another excellent bird watching spot is the Nieuwkoopse Plassen, a large wetland area about 30 minutes from Leiden. This reserve is home to many waterfowl and wading birds, and it's a serene place to spend a day. I took a guided boat tour, which cost €15, and it was amazing to see the birds up close. The visitor center, where you can book tours and get information, is located at Dorpsstraat 116, 2421 BC Nieuwkoop.

For those who prefer to stay closer to the city, the Hortus Botanicus Leiden is a fantastic place to see a variety of bird species. This botanical garden, located at Rapenburg 73, 2311 GJ Leiden, is not only home to beautiful plants but also attracts many birds. I loved sitting in the peaceful garden, listening to the birdsong and spotting different species. Admission to the garden is €7.50 for adults, and it's open year-round.

Personal Reflections

My outdoor adventures in Leiden were some of the most memorable experiences of my trip. The city and its surroundings offer a perfect blend of natural beauty and outdoor activities, making it an ideal destination for nature lovers and adventure seekers. Whether you're hiking through serene nature reserves, kayaking along historic canals, or watching birds in lush wetlands, Leiden provides countless opportunities to connect with nature and enjoy the great outdoors.

One of my favorite memories is an early morning hike in the Boterhuispolder. The mist was rising from the meadows, and the only sounds were the calls of birds and the distant mooing of cows. It was a moment of pure tranquility, and I felt a deep sense of connection to the land. These experiences reminded me of the importance of preserving and respecting nature, and they left me with a profound appreciation for Leiden's natural beauty.

As you plan your visit to Leiden, I encourage you to take advantage of the city's outdoor offerings. Whether you're an avid hiker, a water sports enthusiast, or a casual nature lover, there's something for everyone. And remember, the best adventures are often found off the beaten path, so don't be afraid to explore and discover your own favorite spots in this beautiful part of the Netherlands.

Enjoy your outdoor adventures in Leiden, and may your journey be filled with wonder, discovery, and unforgettable experiences!

Chapter 7

Where to Shop in Leiden

Leiden, the charming university town in the Netherlands, is not only rich in history and culture but also offers a delightful shopping experience. Whether you're looking for unique souvenirs, local crafts, or just a pleasant day of window shopping, Leiden has something for everyone. Having spent a considerable amount of time wandering its streets and markets, I'm excited to share my favorite shopping spots with you. Let's embark on this retail journey together!

Local Markets

Leiden's Weekly Markets: A Vibrant Shopping Experience

Leiden's weekly markets are a must-visit for anyone who enjoys the hustle and bustle of local commerce. The largest and most popular market is held every

Wednesday and Saturday in the heart of the city, along the Nieuwe Rijn and Vismarkt.

Address: Nieuwe Rijn, 2312 JC Leiden

Personal Tip: Arrive early to avoid the crowds and get the best selection of goods. I remember my first visit to this market – the air was filled with the enticing aroma of fresh stroopwafels (thin, caramel-filled waffles) being made on the spot. For around €2, you can indulge in one of these Dutch treats. Don't miss out on the fresh cheese stalls; a small wheel of gouda or edam makes a perfect souvenir.

Notable Stalls:

Cheese Stand: Offering a wide range of locally produced cheeses, including aged gouda which you can get for about €10 per kilogram.

Fish Vendor: Fresh herring and kibbeling (battered and fried fish chunks) for €5 per portion.

Flower Stall: Tulip bulbs, perfect for gardening enthusiasts, costing around €10 for a pack of 20 bulbs.

The Leiden BioMarkt: For Organic Enthusiasts

If you're passionate about organic and sustainable products, the Leiden BioMarkt is your go-to destination. This market operates every Wednesday from 10 AM to 5 PM and offers a variety of organic vegetables, fruits, dairy products, and baked goods.

Address: Vismarkt, 2312 EC Leiden

Personal Experience: I bought a delightful selection of organic honey and fresh bread here. The bread, still warm from the oven, was a steal at €4 per loaf. The vendors are friendly and always willing to share the stories behind their products, which makes the shopping experience even more enriching.

Shopping Streets

Haarlemmerstraat: The Main Shopping Boulevard

Haarlemmerstraat is Leiden's main shopping street, bustling with activity and lined with a mix of high-street brands, boutique stores, and quaint cafés.

Stretching for about a kilometer, this street is perfect for a leisurely shopping stroll.

Address: Haarlemmerstraat, 2312 GE Leiden

Personal Tip: Take your time to explore the smaller side streets and hidden courtyards off Haarlemmerstraat. One of my favorite discoveries was a tiny bookstore called De Kler (Haarlemmerstraat 254, 2312 GE Leiden, Phone: +31 71 514 1450), where I found a fascinating book on Dutch art for €15. Another gem is Bever (Haarlemmerstraat 134, 2312 GH Leiden, Phone: +31 71 514 3077), an outdoor equipment store that has everything you might need for your next adventure.

Breestraat: Combining History with Shopping

Breestraat is another prominent shopping street, rich in history and lined with beautiful old buildings. This street offers a mix of fashion boutiques, antique shops, and gourmet food stores.

Address: Breestraat, 2311 CL Leiden

Personal Experience: On Breestraat, I stumbled upon Van Stockum's Antiquariaat (Breestraat 113, 2311 CL Leiden, Phone: +31 71 514 2770), an antique bookstore with an incredible collection of rare books and maps. It's a treasure trove for history buffs and collectors. I found a vintage map of the Netherlands from the 1800s for €50, a bit pricey, but worth every cent for its historical value.

Souvenirs and Local Crafts

't Leidse Winkeltje: Authentic Leiden Souvenirs

For authentic Leiden souvenirs, 't Leidse Winkeltje is the place to go. This charming shop offers a wide range of local crafts, Delftware (blue and white pottery), and typical Dutch souvenirs.

Address: Nieuwstraat 32, 2312 KC Leiden

Phone: +31 71 513 7998

Personal Tip: I picked up a beautiful hand-painted Delftware vase for €25, which now holds a prominent place in my living room back home. The store also has an excellent selection of traditional Dutch clogs and intricate lacework, perfect for gifts.

De Stelling: Craftsmanship at Its Best

De Stelling is a small, yet remarkable shop where you can find handmade leather goods and unique pieces of jewelry crafted by local artisans. The craftsmanship here is top-notch, and each item tells a story.

Address: Hooglandsekerkgracht 4, 2312 HV Leiden

Phone: +31 71 512 6471

Personal Experience: I bought a beautifully crafted leather wallet for €40. The owner was kind enough to give me a brief history of the shop and even showed me some of the tools they use for leatherworking. It's these personal touches that make shopping in Leiden so special.

Specialty Shops

Gading: Indonesian Treasures

Leiden has a strong connection with Indonesia due to its colonial past, and this is wonderfully reflected in Gading, a shop that offers a variety of Indonesian crafts, textiles, and food products.

Address: Breestraat 97, 2311 CJ Leiden

Phone: +31 71 512 3537

Personal Tip: I couldn't resist buying a traditional batik shirt for €30 and a selection of Indonesian spices for around €10. The shop owner was incredibly knowledgeable and helped me choose spices that would bring authentic Indonesian flavors to my cooking.

Simon Lévelt: A Coffee and Tea Lover's Paradise

If you're a fan of coffee and tea, Simon Lévelt is a must-visit. This specialty store offers an impressive range of high-quality coffees and teas from around the world.

Address: Haarlemmerstraat 67, 2312 DL Leiden

Phone: +31 71 512 4932

Personal Experience: I treated myself to a bag of Ethiopian coffee beans for €12 and a tin of fragrant jasmine tea for €8. The staff were extremely helpful and provided excellent brewing tips. The aroma of freshly ground coffee from this shop is something I will never forget.

Fashion Boutiques

Meijssen Fashion: Contemporary Dutch Style

For contemporary Dutch fashion, Meijssen Fashion is the place to be. This boutique offers a curated selection of stylish clothing and accessories from both local and international designers.

Address: Nieuwe Rijn 28, 2312 JD Leiden

Phone: +31 71 514 1055

Personal Tip: I found a chic coat from a Dutch designer for €120. The quality and design were impeccable, and it's now one of my favorite pieces. The boutique has a welcoming atmosphere, and the staff are always ready to help you find the perfect outfit.

Amacasa: Unique Women's Wear

Amacasa specializes in unique women's wear, with an emphasis on elegant, yet comfortable clothing. This boutique is perfect for finding something special that you won't see everywhere else.

Address: Breestraat 49, 2311 CJ Leiden

Phone: +31 71 513 7721

Personal Experience: I purchased a beautiful silk scarf for €35 and a lovely summer dress for €60. The boutique's cozy interior and friendly staff made the shopping experience delightful.

Practical Tips for Shopping in Leiden

Payment Methods

While most shops in Leiden accept credit and debit cards, it's always a good idea to carry some cash, especially when visiting markets or smaller stores. ATMs are widely available throughout the city.

Tax-Free Shopping

Non-EU visitors can benefit from tax-free shopping in the Netherlands. Look for shops displaying the "Tax-Free" sign and don't forget to ask for your tax-free form at the checkout. You can get a refund on your VAT when you leave the EU.

Opening Hours

Most shops in Leiden are open from 9:00 AM to 6:00 PM, Monday to Saturday. Some shops have extended hours on Thursdays, staying open until 9:00 PM. On Sundays, many shops open from 12:00 PM to 5:00 PM.

Conclusion

Shopping in Leiden is a delightful experience, offering a blend of historical charm and modern convenience. Whether you're exploring the lively markets, browsing the fashionable boutiques on Haarlemmerstraat, or hunting for unique souvenirs in the local craft shops, there's always something new and exciting to discover. My time spent wandering the streets of Leiden, chatting with friendly shopkeepers, and uncovering hidden gems has been incredibly rewarding. I hope this guide helps you make the most of your shopping adventures in this beautiful city. Happy shopping!

Chapter 8

Leiden's Nightlife and Entertainment

Leiden, a charming city in the Netherlands, is not just about picturesque canals and historic buildings. It also boasts a vibrant nightlife that can rival that of much larger cities. During my time in Leiden, I discovered that the evenings here are as lively and captivating as the days. From cozy bars and bustling pubs to energetic nightclubs and sophisticated theatres, there's something for everyone. Let me take you through some of my favorite spots and experiences that made my nights in Leiden unforgettable.

Bars and Pubs

Leiden's bar scene is a delightful mix of traditional Dutch pubs (or "bruine kroegen") and modern bars, each with its own unique atmosphere. One of my favorite spots is Cafe Olivier, located at Hooigracht 23, 2312 KM Leiden. This bar is actually housed in an old church, which gives it a fascinating ambiance. The high ceilings and stained glass windows make it a picturesque place to enjoy a beer. They have an impressive selection of Belgian beers, both on tap and bottled. Prices range from €4 to €7 for a beer, which is quite reasonable given the extensive selection.

Another gem I found is Cafe de Bonte Koe, situated at Hooglandsekerkgracht 37, 2312 HV Leiden. This cozy pub has been around since 1874 and has a very warm, welcoming vibe. The wooden interiors and vintage decor transport you back in time. I particularly enjoyed their selection of local Dutch beers and the friendly conversations with the bartenders, who are more than happy to share stories about the pub's history. A pint here will cost you about €3.50 to €5.

For those who love a good cocktail, Einstein Bar & Café, located at Nieuwe Rijn 19, 2312 JC Leiden, is the place to be. With a terrace overlooking the canal, it's perfect for a relaxed evening. Their cocktail menu is creative and reasonably priced, with most cocktails around €8 to €12. I tried their signature drink, the

"Einstein Mule," which was refreshing and expertly mixed.

Nightclubs

When it comes to nightclubs, Leiden has a few spots that guarantee a great night out. InCasa is one of the most popular clubs in the city, located at Lammermarkt 100, 2312 CW Leiden. It's a versatile venue with different themed nights and events. On Fridays and Saturdays, it turns into a lively dance club with local and international DJs spinning everything from house to techno. The entry fee is typically around €10, and drinks inside range from €3 for a beer to €8 for a cocktail. I had a fantastic time dancing the night away here and met some amazing people.

Another place worth checking out is Next Level, located at Breestraat 170, 2311 CR Leiden. This club is known for its vibrant atmosphere and diverse music genres, from EDM to hip-hop. They often host special events and guest DJs, making every visit unique. The cover charge varies depending on the event, usually between €5 and €15. The energy here is infectious, and it's a great spot if you're looking to party until the early hours of the morning.

Live Music Venues

If live music is more your scene, Leiden has several venues where you can enjoy a variety of performances. Qbus Club, at Middelstegracht 123, 2312 TV Leiden, is a small yet intimate venue that hosts a wide range of live music events. From jazz and blues to indie and rock, there's always something interesting happening. The tickets are reasonably priced, usually between €10 and €20, depending on the artist. I attended a jazz night here, and the cozy setting made it a memorable experience.

Gebr. De Nobel is another fantastic live music venue located at Marktsteeg 4-8, 2312 CS Leiden. This modern venue has two concert halls and hosts both national and international acts. The sound quality here is excellent, and the staff are very friendly. I saw a local indie band perform, and the atmosphere was electric. Ticket prices range from €15 to €40, depending on the event. It's a must-visit for any music lover.

Theatres and Cinemas

Leiden also has a rich cultural scene with several theatres and cinemas that offer a range of entertainment options. Stadsgehoorzaal Leiden, located at Breestraat 60, 2311 CS Leiden, is a historic concert hall that hosts a variety of performances, including classical music, theatre, and dance. The architecture alone is worth the visit. I attended a classical concert here, and the acoustics were superb. Ticket prices vary but generally range from €20 to €50.

For a more contemporary theatre experience, Leidse Schouwburg, at Oude Vest 43, 2312 XS Leiden, offers a diverse program of plays, musicals, and comedy shows. This theatre is the oldest in the Netherlands, dating back to 1705. The intimate setting and high-quality productions make for a great night out. Tickets usually cost between €25 and €60.

When it comes to cinemas, Trianon Theater, located at Breestraat 31, 2311 CJ Leiden, is my favorite. It's an old-school cinema with a charming atmosphere. They show a mix of mainstream and indie films, both in Dutch and English. Tickets are reasonably priced at around €10. I love their cozy seats and the fact that they often have special screenings of classic films.

Personal Reflections

My nights in Leiden were filled with joy and excitement, and each place I visited left a lasting impression. Whether I was enjoying a quiet beer in a historic pub, dancing in a lively nightclub, listening to live music, or watching a play in a beautiful theatre, there was always something to look forward to.

One evening, after a delightful dinner at Olivier, I found myself at Cafe de Bonte Koe. The bartender, an elderly gentleman named Hans, shared fascinating stories about the pub's long history and its role in the local community. As I sipped my beer, I felt a deep connection to the city and its people.

Another memorable night was spent at InCasa, where I danced with locals and fellow travelers until the early hours. The club's vibrant energy and the mix of music genres made it a night to remember. The friends I made there and the memories we created will always hold a special place in my heart.

Attending a jazz night at Qbus Club was another highlight. The intimate setting allowed me to fully immerse myself in the music, and the talented musicians transported me to another world. It was a night of pure musical bliss.

In conclusion, Leiden's nightlife and entertainment scene offers a wealth of experiences for every type of traveler. Whether you're looking for a relaxed evening in a cozy pub, a night of dancing in a lively club, an intimate live music performance, or a cultural experience in a historic theatre, Leiden has it all. As you explore this enchanting city, make sure to immerse yourself in its vibrant nightlife and create your own unforgettable memories.

Chapter 9

What to Do and Not to Do in Leiden

A h, Leiden! The city where the past and present seamlessly blend, where charming canals weave through historic streets, and where you can feel the whispers of history with every step you take. During my time in Leiden, I was enchanted by its rich heritage, vibrant culture, and the friendly locals who welcomed me with open arms. However, like any traveler, I learned a few things about what to do and what not to do to ensure a smooth and respectful visit. Let me share my experiences and tips to help you make the most of your trip to this beautiful Dutch city.

Respecting Local Customs and Traditions

Embracing Dutch Directness

One of the first things I noticed in Leiden, and in the Netherlands in general, is the Dutch directness. The locals are straightforward and honest, which might come off as blunt to some. However, I found this refreshing. When asking for directions or recommendations, expect clear and to-the-point answers. There's no need to beat around the bush!

Personal Tip: If you're not used to this level of directness, don't take it personally. It's just the Dutch way of being efficient and honest. I once asked a local where I could find the best stroopwafels, and they bluntly told me, "Not here, go to the market in Gouda." It turned out to be the best advice ever!

Mind Your Bicycle Etiquette

Leiden, like the rest of the Netherlands, is a cyclist's paradise. Bicycles are the primary mode of transport, and there are more bikes than people! While cycling is a great way to explore the city, it's important to follow the local bike etiquette.

Personal Tip: Always use bike lanes, signal your turns, and never walk on bike paths. I learned this the hard way when I absentmindedly wandered onto a bike lane and nearly caused a pile-up. Also, lock your bike securely with a sturdy lock, as bike theft can be an issue.

Respecting Quiet Hours

Leiden is home to many students, given its prestigious Leiden University, but it's also a place where locals appreciate their peace and quiet, especially in residential areas. The Dutch value tranquility, particularly in the evenings.

Personal Tip: Keep noise levels down after 10 PM, especially if you're staying in a residential area. During my stay, I once hosted a late-night gathering at my Airbnb, and the polite knock from the neighbor was a gentle reminder of this custom.

Safety Tips

Navigating the Canals Safely

The canals of Leiden are picturesque and perfect for a leisurely boat ride. However, safety is key. The canals can be deeper than they appear, and the edges can be slippery.

Personal Tip: Always be cautious near the edges, especially at night. If you plan on boating, wear a life jacket and ensure you're familiar with basic boating rules. I once almost lost my balance while trying to take a selfie on a narrow canal bridge—lesson learned!

Staying Safe in Crowded Areas

Leiden's markets, like the famous Wednesday and Saturday market on the Nieuwe Rijn, are bustling and vibrant. However, crowded areas can be prime spots for pickpockets.

Personal Tip: Keep your belongings secure. Use a crossbody bag and keep it in front of you. I always kept my valuables in a zipped bag and stayed alert, which saved me from any potential mishaps.

Emergency Numbers

It's always good to have local emergency numbers handy. In the Netherlands, the general emergency number is 112. For non-emergencies, you can contact the local police at 0900-8844.

Common Tourist Mistakes

Underestimating the Weather

Dutch weather can be unpredictable. One moment it's sunny, and the next, you're caught in a sudden downpour. I made the rookie mistake of not checking the weather forecast regularly.

Personal Tip: Always carry an umbrella or a raincoat, and dress in layers. I remember getting soaked to the bone on a day I thought would be perfectly sunny. Now, I always check the weather app first thing in the morning.

Not Exploring Beyond the Main Attractions

Leiden is brimming with hidden gems beyond its famous sites like the Rijksmuseum van Oudheden or the Hortus Botanicus. Many tourists stick to the main attractions and miss out on the lesser-known delights.

Personal Tip: Venture off the beaten path. Explore the quaint streets, discover local cafes, and visit smaller museums. One of my favorite finds was the Museum Boerhaave, a fascinating museum dedicated to the history of science and medicine, with an entrance fee of just €10.

Ignoring Public Transportation Options

Leiden's compact size makes it walkable, but don't overlook its efficient public transport system. Buses and trains are convenient and can save you time and energy.

Personal Tip: Get an OV-chipkaart for hassle-free travel on public transport. I found the buses particularly useful when I wanted to visit the outskirts or had a long day of exploring.

Responsible Tourism

Supporting Local Businesses

Tourism is vital for Leiden's economy, and supporting local businesses can make a big difference. From family-owned restaurants to artisanal shops, there are plenty of opportunities to contribute positively to the local community.

Personal Tip: Skip the chain stores and eat at local restaurants. My favorite was 'Het Prentenkabinet', a charming restaurant located at Kloksteeg 25. Their traditional Dutch dishes with a modern twist were worth every euro.

Environmental Responsibility

Leiden is known for its beautiful landscapes and clean environment. As a responsible tourist, it's important to minimize your environmental impact.

Personal Tip: Dispose of your trash properly and recycle when possible. Most public places have separate bins for recycling. Also, consider renting a bike instead of a car to reduce your carbon footprint. Cycling not only helps the environment but also offers a unique way to explore the city.

Respecting Heritage Sites

Leiden is a city rich in history, with many heritage sites that require preservation. Treat these sites with respect to ensure they remain intact for future generations.

Personal Tip: Avoid touching artifacts in museums and refrain from taking flash photography where prohibited. When I visited the Pieterskerk, I was mindful to stay within designated areas and follow all guidelines provided by the staff.

Enjoying Leiden Like a Local

Attend Local Events

Leiden hosts numerous local events and festivals that provide a deeper insight into Dutch culture. One of the highlights during my stay was the 'Leidens Ontzet' (Leiden's Relief), celebrated every year on October 3rd. This festival commemorates the end of the Spanish siege in 1574 and includes parades, music, and traditional herring and white bread.

Personal Tip: Check the local event calendar to see what's happening during your visit. Participating in local festivities can be a highlight of your trip. During Leidens Ontzet, I joined the locals in the festivities, tasted the traditional food, and even tried my hand at some Dutch folk dances!

Learn Basic Dutch Phrases

While most people in Leiden speak excellent English, learning a few basic Dutch phrases can enhance your experience and show respect to the locals.

Personal Tip: Simple phrases like "Dank u wel" (Thank you) and "Alstublieft" (Please) can go a long way. I found that attempting to speak Dutch often resulted in warm smiles and friendly responses. The locals appreciate the effort!

Enjoying the Canal Life

The canals are the lifeblood of Leiden, offering a unique perspective of the city. Taking a boat tour is a must, but don't just stick to the commercial tours. Rent a small boat and explore at your own pace.

Personal Tip: Boat rentals are available at several locations, such as Bootjes en Broodjes located at Apothekersdijk 5. Prices start at around €25 per hour. I rented a boat for an afternoon and it was one of the most serene and enjoyable experiences of my trip. Gliding through the canals, passing historic buildings and waving at locals was simply magical.

Savoring Dutch Delicacies

No trip to Leiden is complete without indulging in some traditional Dutch cuisine. From street food to fine dining, the city offers a range of delicious options.

Personal Tip: Try the local specialties like herring, stroopwafels, and bitterballen. The Wednesday and

Saturday market at Nieuwe Rijn is a great place to sample these treats. I vividly remember my first taste of fresh herring at the market – it was an unexpected delight that I quickly grew fond of!

Respecting Bicycle Culture

As I mentioned before, cycling is a way of life in Leiden. It's not just about transportation; it's a cultural experience. Respecting this culture means understanding and following the unwritten rules.

Personal Tip: Always yield to cyclists, even if you're walking. Use the designated pedestrian crossings and stay off the bike paths. Renting a bike is also a great way to fit in and explore like a local. My bike rental from 'Rent-a-Bike Leiden' at Lange Mare 65 cost around €10 per day, and it was worth every cent.

Appreciating Leiden's Green Spaces

Leiden is blessed with beautiful parks and gardens. Hortus Botanicus, one of the oldest botanical gardens in the world, is a must-visit.

Personal Tip: Spend a leisurely afternoon in Hortus Botanicus, located at Rapenburg 73. The entrance fee is around €8, and it's a peaceful oasis in the heart of the city. I loved wandering through the tropical greenhouses and sitting by the tranquil ponds.

Conclusion

Leiden is a city that captures the heart and soul of anyone who visits. From its historic canals and vibrant markets to its rich cultural traditions and friendly locals, there's so much to see and do. By respecting local customs, staying safe, avoiding common tourist mistakes, and embracing responsible tourism, you'll ensure that your visit is not only enjoyable but also respectful and enriching.

During my time in Leiden, I felt like I was living in a charming storybook, filled with delightful surprises and memorable experiences. I hope my insights and tips help you create your own unforgettable adventure in this beautiful Dutch city. Safe travels, and enjoy every moment in Leiden!

Chapter 10

Itineraries and Sample Plans

When planning a trip to Leiden, having a well-thought-out itinerary can make all the difference. As someone who has spent a significant amount of time exploring this enchanting city, I can assure you that Leiden has something for everyone. Whether you're here for a quick weekend getaway, a deep cultural immersion, an outdoor adventure, a family-friendly trip, or a budget travel experience, Leiden has it all. Let me walk you through some sample itineraries to ensure you have an unforgettable stay.

Weekend Getaway

If you only have a weekend to explore Leiden, don't worry. You can still experience the essence of this beautiful city.

Day 1: Arrival and Initial Exploration

Morning:

Arrive in Leiden: Whether you fly into Amsterdam Schiphol Airport (a 20-minute train ride to Leiden) or come by train from another part of the Netherlands, arriving early will give you a full day to start your adventure.

Check-in: Stay at Boutique Hotel d'Oude Morsch, located at Park de Put 1, 2312 BM Leiden. This charming hotel is housed in a historic building and offers rooms starting at €120 per night. Phone: +31 71 260 1260.

Afternoon:

Lunch at Annie's: Located at Hoogstraat 1a, 2312 JA Leiden, Annie's is a delightful spot by the water. Enjoy a sandwich or salad for around €15. Phone: +31 71 512 1530.

Explore the Old Observatory: Take a leisurely walk to the Old Observatory at Sterrenwachtlaan 11, 2311 GP Leiden. Entry is €7.50. This is the oldest remaining university observatory in the world and offers beautiful views and fascinating exhibits. Phone: +31 71 527 5789.

Evening:

Dinner at Puur Eten & Drinken: This restaurant, located at Stationsweg 1, 2312 AW Leiden, offers local and organic dishes. Expect to spend around €25-€30 per person. Phone: +31 71 514 2860.

Stroll along the Canals: End your evening with a peaceful walk along Leiden's picturesque canals, soaking in the city's night-time charm.

Day 2: Museums and Gardens

Morning:

Breakfast at the Hotel: Enjoy a hearty breakfast at Boutique Hotel d'Oude Morsch.

Visit the Rijksmuseum van Oudheden: Located at Rapenburg 28, 2311 EW Leiden, this national museum of antiquities is a must-see. Entry is €12.50. Phone: +31 71 516 3163.

Afternoon:

Lunch at Bagels & Beans: Located at Haarlemmerstraat 38, 2312 GA Leiden, this cozy café offers a variety of bagels and salads for around €10-€15. Phone: +31 71 514 0260.

Stroll through the Hortus Botanicus: Visit the Hortus Botanicus at Rapenburg 73, 2311 GJ Leiden. Entry is €8.50. This stunning botanical garden is perfect for an afternoon of relaxation and exploration. Phone: +31 71 527 7249.

Evening:

Dinner at La Plancha: Located at Noordeinde 23, 2311 CA Leiden, this Spanish tapas restaurant offers a variety of delicious dishes. Expect to spend around €30 per person. Phone: +31 71 513 3737.

Relax at the Hotel: After dinner, unwind at the hotel and prepare for your departure the next day.

Cultural Immersion

Leiden is a city rich in history and culture. If you're here to immerse yourself in the local culture, this itinerary is for you.

Day 1: Historical Landmarks

Morning:

Arrive and Check-in: Stay at the Steenhof Suites, located at Steenstraat 1, 2312 BS Leiden. Rooms start at €140 per night. Phone: +31 71 240 7000.

Visit the Pieterskerk: Located at Kloksteeg 16, 2311 SL Leiden, this church is a historical landmark with stunning architecture. Entry is €5. Phone: +31 71 512 4140.

Afternoon:

Lunch at Waag: This restaurant, located at Aalmarkt 21, 2311 EC Leiden, offers a variety of Dutch dishes. Expect to spend around €20. Phone: +31 71 514 3388.

Explore the Museum De Lakenhal: Located at Oude Singel 28-32, 2312 RA Leiden, this museum offers a fascinating look into Leiden's artistic and cultural history. Entry is €12. Phone: +31 71 516 5360.

Evening:

Dinner at The Bishop: Located at Bargelaan 180, 2333 CW Leiden, this restaurant offers a fine dining experience with dishes starting at €30. Phone: +31 71 203 2474.

Evening Walk: Take an evening walk through the historic center, admiring the architecture and atmosphere.

Day 2: Art and Academia

Morning:

Breakfast at the Hotel: Enjoy a continental breakfast at Steenhof Suites.

Visit the Leiden American Pilgrim Museum: Located at Beschuitsteeg 9, 2312 JT Leiden, this small museum offers a unique glimpse into the lives of the Pilgrims before they left for America. Entry is €9. Phone: +31 71 512 2413.

Afternoon:

Lunch at Oudt Leyden: Located at Steenstraat 49, 2312 BP Leiden, this restaurant is famous for its traditional Dutch pancakes. Expect to spend around €15-€20. Phone: +31 71 513 3144.

Explore the Boerhaave Museum: Located at Lange St. Agnietenstraat 10, 2312 WC Leiden, this museum is dedicated to the history of science and medicine. Entry is €14. Phone: +31 71 751 9999.

Evening:

Dinner at De Bonte Koe: Located at Kaasmarkt 1, 2312 HZ Leiden, this charming restaurant offers a variety of Dutch and international dishes. Expect to spend around €25-€30. Phone: +31 71 512 1177.

Relax at the Hotel: After a day of cultural exploration, relax at the hotel and reflect on your experiences.

Outdoor Adventure

For those who love the great outdoors, Leiden offers plenty of opportunities for adventure.

Day 1: Parks and Waterways

Morning:

Arrive and Check-in: Stay at City Hotel Nieuw Minerva, located at Boommarkt 23, 2311 EA Leiden. Rooms start at €110 per night. Phone: +31 71 512 6358.

Visit the Leidse Hout: Start your adventure with a visit to this beautiful park located at Houtlaan 100, 2334 CL Leiden. It's perfect for a morning hike or a relaxing walk. Entry is free. Phone: +31 71 513 1960.

Afternoon:

Lunch at Het Prentenkabinet: Located at Kloksteeg 25, 2311 SK Leiden, this restaurant offers a lovely garden setting. Expect to spend around €20-€25. Phone: +31 71 512 6669.

Kayaking on the Canals: Rent a kayak from Bootjes en Broodjes, located at Blauwpoortsbrug 1, 2312 GA Leiden. Prices start at €15 per hour. Phone: +31 71 513 4939.

Evening:

Dinner at De Gaanderij: Located at Doelensteeg 8, 2311 VL Leiden, this restaurant offers a cozy atmosphere with delicious dishes. Expect to spend around €30 per person. Phone: +31 71 513 8615.

Evening Stroll: Enjoy an evening stroll along the canals, taking in the serene beauty of Leiden at night.

Day 2: Nature Reserves and Cycling

Morning:

Breakfast at the Hotel: Enjoy a hearty breakfast at City Hotel Nieuw Minerva.

Visit the Kagerplassen: Take a short trip to the Kagerplassen, a beautiful lake area perfect for a morning of sailing or paddleboarding. Rentals are available at Jachthaven Poelgeest, located at Oegstgeesterweg 209, 2231 AZ Rijnsburg. Prices start at €20 per hour. Phone: +31 71 519 1929.

Afternoon:

Lunch at Brasserie Park: Located at Van Diepeningenlaan 2, 2352 KA Leiderdorp, this brasserie offers a variety of tasty dishes. Expect to spend around €20-€25. Phone: +31 71 589 8822.

Cycling Tour: Rent a bike from EasyFiets, located at Steenstraat 2, 2312 BS Leiden. Prices start at €10 per day. Phone: +31 71 514 8785. Explore the scenic cycling routes around Leiden, including the beautiful route to the nearby beach.

Evening:

Dinner at Scarlatti: Located at Nieuwe Rijn 36, 2312 JH Leiden, this restaurant offers a great dining experience with dishes starting at €25. Phone: +31 71 513 0668.

Relax at the Hotel: After an active day, unwind at the hotel and prepare for your departure the next day.

Family-Friendly Trip

Leiden is a fantastic destination for families, offering a range of activities that both kids and adults will enjoy.

Day 1: Interactive Museums and Parks

Morning:

Arrive and Check-in: Stay at Holiday Inn Leiden, located at Haagse Schouwweg 10, 2332 KG Leiden. Family rooms start at €140 per night. Phone: +31 71 535 5555.

Visit CORPUS: Located at Willem Einthovenstraat 1, 2342 BH Oegstgeest, this interactive museum takes you on a journey through the human body. It's both educational and fun for kids. Entry is €18.95 for adults and €16.95 for children. Phone: +31 71 751 0200.

Afternoon:

Lunch at Restaurant Woods: Located at Haagweg 81, 2321 AA Leiden, this restaurant offers a kid-friendly menu. Expect to spend around €20-€25. Phone: +31 71 521 9174.

Explore the Naturalis Biodiversity Center: Located at Darwinweg 2, 2333 CR Leiden, this natural history museum is a hit with kids. Entry is €16 for adults and €11 for children. Phone: +31 71 751 2345.

Evening:

Dinner at Restaurant The Bishop: Located at Bargelaan 180, 2333 CW Leiden, this restaurant offers a variety of dishes to suit all tastes. Expect to spend around €25-€30 per person. Phone: +31 71 203 2474.

Evening Walk: Take a family-friendly walk along the canals before heading back to the hotel.

Day 2: Playgrounds and Picnics

Morning:

Breakfast at the Hotel: Enjoy a continental breakfast at Holiday Inn Leiden.

Visit the Molen de Valk Windmill Museum: Located at 2e Binnenvestgracht 1, 2312 BZ Leiden, this windmill museum is fascinating for kids and adults alike. Entry is €5 for adults and €2.50 for children. Phone: +31 71 516 5353.

Afternoon:

Lunch at Stadscafé Van der Werff: Located at Steenstraat 2, 2312 BS Leiden, this café offers a relaxed atmosphere and kid-friendly meals. Expect to spend around €15-€20. Phone: +31 71 514 8785.

Playtime at Vlietland: This recreational area, located at Rietpolderweg 11, 2266 BM Leidschendam, is perfect for a family picnic and outdoor activities. Entry is free. Phone: +31 71 561 4949.

Evening:

Dinner at De Beukenhof: Located at Terweeweg 2-4, 2341 CR Oegstgeest, this restaurant offers a delightful dining experience with dishes starting at €30. Phone: +31 71 517 3196.

Relax at the Hotel: After a fun-filled day, unwind at the hotel and prepare for your departure the next day.

Budget Travel

Leiden can be a budget-friendly destination if you know where to go and what to do. Here's how to enjoy Leiden without breaking the bank.

Day 1: Affordable Exploration

Morning:

Arrive and Check-in: Stay at Ibis Leiden Centre, located at Stationsplein 240-242, 2312 AR Leiden. Rooms start at €80 per night. Phone: +31 71 516 0000.

Free Walking Tour: Start your day with a free walking tour of Leiden. The tours usually start from the Leiden Centraal Station and offer a great introduction to the city's history and main attractions. Remember to tip your guide!

Afternoon:

Lunch at HEMA: Located at Haarlemmerstraat 131, 2312 DT Leiden, HEMA offers affordable sandwiches and snacks. Expect to spend around €5-€10. Phone: +31 71 513 3797.

Visit the Leiden University Library: Located at Witte Singel 27, 2311 BG Leiden, this library is free to enter and offers a peaceful place to relax and read. Phone: +31 71 527 2832.

Evening:

Dinner at Taco Mundo: Located at Breestraat 113, 2311 CL Leiden, this restaurant offers affordable Mexican food. Expect to spend around €10-€15. Phone: +31 71 514 5690.

Evening Walk: Enjoy a free evening walk along the canals and through the historic center.

Day 2: Low-Cost Attractions and Activities

Morning:

Breakfast at the Hotel: Enjoy a simple breakfast at Ibis Leiden Centre.

Visit the Molenmuseum de Valk: Located at 2e Binnenvestgracht 1, 2312 BZ Leiden, this windmill museum offers affordable entry at €5 for adults and €2.50 for children. Phone: +31 71 516 5353.

Afternoon:

Lunch at the Markt: Visit the weekly market (held on Wednesdays and Saturdays) at Nieuwe Rijn and buy affordable and delicious local foods. Expect to spend around €10-€15.

Explore the Leiden Botanical Garden: Located at Rapenburg 73, 2311 GJ Leiden, entry is €8.50. Enjoy a relaxing afternoon in this beautiful garden. Phone: +31 71 527 7249.

Evening:

Dinner at Eazie: Located at Steenstraat 40, 2312 CL Leiden, Eazie offers healthy and affordable Asian meals. Expect to spend around €10-€15. Phone: +31 71 514 0469.

Relax at the Hotel: After a budget-friendly day, unwind at the hotel and prepare for your departure the next day.

These itineraries are designed to give you a comprehensive and enjoyable experience in Leiden, no matter your travel style or budget. Whether you're here for a quick weekend, a deep cultural dive, an outdoor adventure, a family trip, or a budget-friendly escape, Leiden has something to offer. Enjoy your stay, and make the most of this charming Dutch city!

Chapter 11

Where to Stay in Leiden

Overview of Accommodation Options

Leiden, often referred to as the "Key City" due to its historical significance and its emblem featuring keys, offers a diverse range of accommodations to suit every traveler's needs. During my time exploring this charming Dutch city, I had the pleasure of experiencing a variety of lodging options, each with its unique charm and appeal. From luxurious resorts to budget-friendly hotels, quaint boutique guesthouses, and unique stays, Leiden has something for everyone.

Luxury Resorts

Hotel van der Valk Leiden: Elegance and Comfort

During my stay in Leiden, I had the pleasure of experiencing the elegance and comfort of the Hotel van der Valk. This luxurious resort is situated just outside the city center, offering a tranquil retreat while still being conveniently close to the main attractions. The hotel boasts modern amenities, spacious rooms, and excellent service.

Address: Haagse Schouwweg 14, 2332 KG Leiden

Phone: +31 71 573 1731

Personal Experience: I spent a weekend here, and it was absolutely delightful. The rooms were spacious, with large windows offering beautiful views of the surrounding greenery. The restaurant served delectable Dutch and international cuisine, with dishes ranging from €20 to €35. Don't miss their breakfast buffet, priced at €18.50, which offers a wide variety of fresh and delicious options.

Huys van Leyden: A Historical Gem

For those who prefer a blend of luxury and history, Huys van Leyden is a perfect choice. This boutique hotel is located in a beautifully restored 17th-century building in the heart of Leiden. The interiors are tastefully decorated, combining historical charm with modern comforts.

Address: Oude Singel 212, 2312 RJ Leiden

Phone: +31 71 513 1962

Personal Experience: Staying at Huys van Leyden felt like stepping back in time, with its antique furnishings and historical ambiance. The staff was incredibly welcoming and attentive. My room, which cost around €150 per night, had a cozy fireplace and a stunning canal view. The highlight was their private wellness center, where I enjoyed a relaxing sauna session.

Budget-Friendly Hotels

Ibis Leiden Centre: Convenience on a Budget

If you're looking for a budget-friendly option without compromising on comfort, Ibis Leiden Centre is an excellent choice. Located right next to the Leiden Central Station, this hotel offers easy access to the city's attractions and public transport.

Address: Stationsplein 240, 2312 AR Leiden

Phone: +31 71 516 0000

Personal Experience: I stayed here for a few nights and found it extremely convenient. The rooms were small but clean and comfortable, with prices starting at €75 per night. The buffet breakfast, priced at €14, was quite good, offering a variety of options to start the day.

Hotel Mayflower: Central and Affordable

Hotel Mayflower is another great budget option, centrally located near the bustling Beestenmarkt and close to many of Leiden's attractions. This family-run hotel offers friendly service and comfortable rooms at affordable prices.

Address: Beestenmarkt 2, 2312 CC Leiden

Phone: +31 71 512 3231

Personal Experience: My room was simple but cozy, with a nightly rate of around €80. The hotel's location was fantastic, allowing me to explore the city center on foot easily. I particularly enjoyed the nearby cafes and restaurants, which added to the vibrant atmosphere.

Boutique Guesthouses

Steenhof Suites: Charming and Cozy

Steenhof Suites offers a unique boutique experience in a beautifully restored historic building. Each suite is individually decorated, providing a charming and cozy atmosphere with modern amenities.

Address: Steenstraat 1, 2312 BS Leiden

Phone: +31 71 576 0915

Personal Experience: My suite was beautifully decorated with a mix of vintage and contemporary furnishings. Priced at around €160 per night, it included a small kitchenette and a luxurious bathroom with a rainfall shower. The staff was incredibly friendly and helpful, making my stay even more enjoyable.

Boutique Hotel d'Oude Morsch: A Piece of History

Located in a former military barracks, Boutique Hotel d'Oude Morsch is a charming boutique hotel with a rich history. The hotel's unique setting and stylish interiors make it a memorable place to stay.

Address: Park de Put 1, 2312 BM Leiden

Phone: +31 71 303 0630

Personal Experience: Staying at this hotel was a unique experience. My room, costing around €140 per night, was spacious and tastefully decorated. The hotel's restaurant served delicious meals, with dinner prices ranging from €20 to €40. I particularly loved the outdoor terrace, which offered a lovely spot to relax with a glass of wine.

Unique Stays

Boat Hotel De Barones van Leyden: Stay on the Water

For a truly unique experience, consider staying at Boat Hotel De Barones van Leyden. This floating hotel offers charming rooms on a historic barge moored in one of Leiden's picturesque canals.

Address: Apothekersdijk 5, 2312 DD Leiden

Phone: +31 71 514 3384

Personal Experience: I stayed here for two nights, and it was a magical experience. The gentle rocking of the boat and the sound of water made for a peaceful night's sleep. My room, priced at €180 per night, was cozy and well-equipped. Breakfast, served on deck, was a highlight, with prices at €17.50.

Villa Rameau: A Historic Hideaway

Villa Rameau offers a unique stay in a beautifully restored 16th-century building. Located in the heart of Leiden, this historic villa provides an intimate and luxurious experience.

Address: Kloksteeg 16, 2311 SK Leiden

Phone: +31 71 513 1962

Personal Experience: My stay at Villa Rameau was nothing short of extraordinary. The villa, which I rented for €300 per night, was a blend of historical charm and modern luxury. It had a fully equipped kitchen, a spacious living area, and a private garden. It felt like having my own little piece of history in the heart of Leiden.

Conclusion

Leiden's diverse range of accommodations ensures that every traveler can find the perfect place to stay, whether you're looking for luxury, comfort, or a unique experience. My time in this charming city was made even more memorable by the wonderful places I stayed, each offering its own special touch and hospitality. As you plan your visit to Leiden, consider these options to enhance your travel experience and create lasting memories. Safe travels, and enjoy your stay in this beautiful city!

Chapter 12

Top Recommended Hotels and Resorts

Finding the perfect place to stay is a crucial part of any trip, and my time in Leiden was no different. I had the pleasure of experiencing various accommodations that catered to different needs and preferences. Whether you're seeking luxury, traveling on a budget, planning a family vacation, or looking for a romantic getaway, Leiden has something to offer. Here are my top recommendations based on personal experience.

Best for Luxury

When I wanted to treat myself to an opulent stay, the Boutique Hotel d'Oude Morsch was my go-to choice. Nestled in the heart of the city, this hotel is housed in a beautifully renovated old military barrack. The blend of historical charm and modern amenities made my stay unforgettable.

Address: Park de Put 1, 2312 BM Leiden

Phone: +31 71 744 0052

From the moment I walked in, the staff treated me like royalty. The rooms are spacious and elegantly decorated, featuring luxurious linens, plush furnishings, and stunning views of the surrounding park and canal. I particularly enjoyed the suite with a private terrace, perfect for enjoying a quiet evening with a glass of wine.

Price: Rooms start at €200 per night, but it's worth every euro for the experience.

The hotel's restaurant serves a delightful breakfast with fresh, local ingredients. Their à la carte dinner menu was also a highlight, offering gourmet dishes that were both delicious and beautifully presented.

Best for Budget

For those traveling on a budget, I found the Ibis Leiden Centre to be an excellent choice. It's conveniently located right next to the Leiden Central Station, making it easy to explore the city and beyond.

Address: Stationsplein 240-242, 2312 AR Leiden

Phone: +31 71 516 0000

Despite being a budget-friendly hotel, the Ibis Leiden Centre doesn't compromise on comfort or quality. The rooms are clean, modern, and well-equipped with everything you need for a pleasant stay. I appreciated the comfortable bed and the soundproof windows, which ensured a good night's sleep even with the hustle and bustle of the nearby station.

Price: Rooms typically start at €75 per night, making it a great deal for budget-conscious travelers.

The hotel offers a decent breakfast buffet for an additional fee, but I often opted to grab a pastry and coffee from one of the nearby bakeries for a more authentic Dutch experience.

Best for Families

Traveling with family requires a bit more space and convenience, and the Holiday Inn Leiden fits the bill perfectly. This hotel is located a bit outside the city center, but it's well-connected by public transport and offers plenty of amenities to keep everyone entertained.

Address: Haagse Schouwweg 10, 2332 KG Leiden

Phone: +31 71 535 5555

The family rooms here are fantastic, offering ample space and all the necessary amenities. My kids loved the indoor pool and the play area, while my spouse and I appreciated the fitness center and sauna. The hotel also has a charming courtyard where we enjoyed some downtime.

Price: Family rooms start at around €130 per night.

One of the best features of this hotel is the on-site restaurant, which offers a kid-friendly menu and a buffet with a variety of options to suit all tastes. The breakfast buffet, included in our stay, was a hit with everyone, providing a great start to our busy days exploring Leiden.

Best for Couples

For a romantic getaway, I highly recommend the Huys van Leyden. This boutique hotel is set in a beautifully restored 17th-century building, offering an intimate and charming atmosphere perfect for couples.

Address: Oude Singel 212, 2312 RJ Leiden

Phone: +31 71 260 1400

Our room was exquisitely decorated with antique furnishings and modern comforts, creating a cozy and romantic setting. The staff went out of their way to make our stay special, even arranging for a bottle of champagne and chocolates upon our arrival.

Price: Rooms for couples start at €180 per night, with various packages available for special occasions.

One of the highlights of our stay was the private sauna and jacuzzi, available for booking. It was the perfect way to unwind after a day of sightseeing. We also enjoyed a delicious breakfast served in our room, adding to the luxurious and romantic experience.

Personal Reflections

Staying in these various accommodations allowed me to experience different facets of Leiden. Each place had its unique charm and advantages, catering to different needs and preferences. Whether I was indulging in luxury, sticking to a budget, enjoying family time, or savoring a romantic escape, Leiden offered the perfect home away from home.

One of my favorite memories was from my stay at Boutique Hotel d'Oude Morsch. After a long day of exploring the city's museums and canals, I returned to my suite to find the bed turned down with a small chocolate on the pillow and a note wishing me a pleasant evening. It's the small touches like these that make a stay truly special.

At Ibis Leiden Centre, I loved the convenience of being able to hop on a train and visit nearby cities like The Hague and Amsterdam. Despite the hotel's budget status, the staff was always friendly and helpful, making my stay comfortable and enjoyable.

The Holiday Inn Leiden provided a perfect balance of relaxation and entertainment for my family. I remember the joy on my kids' faces as they splashed in the pool, and the peaceful moments my spouse and I enjoyed in the sauna.

Huys van Leyden, with its historical charm and modern luxury, was the ideal setting for a romantic getaway. The private sauna session was a highlight, offering a serene and intimate escape from the busy tourist spots.

In conclusion, Leiden's diverse range of accommodations ensures that every traveler can find a perfect fit. From luxurious boutique hotels to budget-friendly options, family-oriented stays, and romantic hideaways, each place adds a unique flavor to the Leiden experience. So, whether you're planning your first visit or returning for another adventure, rest assured that Leiden has the perfect place for you to stay and create lasting memories.

Chapter 13

How to Choose the Right Accommodation in Leiden, Netherlands

Finding the perfect place to stay can make or break your travel experience. During my time in Leiden, a city steeped in history and charm, I discovered that choosing the right accommodation involves several important considerations. From understanding your own needs to researching the best locations and amenities, here are my insights and tips to help you make an informed decision.

Factors to Consider

Understanding Your Needs and Preferences

Before you even start looking at hotels or Airbnb listings, it's crucial to understand what you need and prefer. Are you traveling alone, with a partner, or with family? Do you prefer a cozy bed and breakfast, a luxurious hotel, or perhaps a budget-friendly hostel? Here are a few factors to think about:

Budget: Determine how much you're willing to spend per night. Leiden offers a range of accommodations from budget to luxury.

Length of Stay: For longer stays, consider places with kitchen facilities or laundry services.

Type of Experience: Are you looking for a historical experience, a modern stay, or something quirky and unique?

Travel Purpose: If you're here for leisure, proximity to attractions might be important. If it's for business, you might prioritize a place with a reliable internet connection and workspaces.

Location and Proximity

Leiden is a compact city, but where you stay can significantly influence your experience. The city is divided into several distinct areas, each with its own charm and conveniences.

City Center: Staying in the city center means you're close to major attractions like the Rijksmuseum van Oudheden and the Leiden University. It's bustling and vibrant, perfect if you enjoy being in the heart of the action.

Personal Experience: I stayed at the Hotel De Doelen once, a charming historic hotel on Rapenburg 2, right next to the university. It was priced around €120 per night. The proximity to cafes and museums was unbeatable.

Station Area: If you plan on making day trips to nearby cities like Amsterdam or The Hague, staying near Leiden Central Station might be convenient.

Personal Experience: I found Hotel Mayflower, located at Beestenmarkt 2, very practical. It was about €95 per night and just a five-minute walk from the station.

Outskirts: For a quieter stay, consider accommodations on the outskirts. This can offer a more relaxed atmosphere and often more affordable options.

Location and Amenities

Central and Convenient Locations

When it comes to choosing the right location, convenience is key. You'll want to be near public transport, restaurants, and major attractions. Here's a breakdown of what to look for in different areas of Leiden:

Near Public Transport: Staying close to bus stops or the train station makes it easy to explore not only Leiden but also neighboring cities.

Hotel Nieuw Minerva: Located at Boommarkt 23, it's a beautiful hotel in the city center, close to public transport. Prices start at €110 per night.

Historical Sights: If you're a history buff, opt for accommodations near museums and historical sites.

Boutique Hotel d'Oude Morsch: This hotel, at Park de Put 1, is a former military barracks turned boutique hotel, located near the Museum of Ethnology. It's a bit pricier, around €150 per night, but worth every penny for history enthusiasts.

Dining and Nightlife: For food lovers, staying near Pieterskerk-Choorsteeg offers a plethora of dining options.

Bree33: Located at Breestraat 33, this hotel is surrounded by great eateries and cafes. Rooms start at €100 per night.

Essential Amenities

Different travelers prioritize different amenities, so it's essential to know what you need. Here are some amenities to consider:

Wi-Fi: Crucial for both leisure and business travelers.

Breakfast: Some hotels offer complimentary breakfast, which can be a great start to your day.

Personal Experience: I stayed at Boutique Hotel Ex Libris at Kloksteeg 4, where a sumptuous breakfast was included in the €130 per night rate.

Parking: If you're renting a car, ensure the hotel offers parking facilities.

Fitness Center: For those who like to stay active while traveling.

Laundry Services: Handy for longer stays.

Pet-Friendly: If you're traveling with pets, make sure the accommodation is pet-friendly.

Reading Reviews

One of the best ways to ensure you're choosing the right accommodation is to read reviews from other travelers. Websites like TripAdvisor, Booking.com, and Google Reviews offer a wealth of information. Here's how to make the most of them:

Look for Recent Reviews: These provide the most current information.

Check for Consistent Complaints: If multiple reviews mention the same issue, it's likely a legitimate concern.

Consider Reviewer Demographics: Reviews from travelers similar to you (solo, family, business) can be more relevant.

Photos: User-uploaded photos give a more accurate depiction than professional shots.

Personal Recommendations

During my time in Leiden, I had the opportunity to stay in various accommodations and also received recommendations from locals and fellow travelers. Here are a few top picks:

Luxury Stay: Villa Beukenhof at Terweeweg 2-4 is a luxurious choice. With its historic charm and modern amenities, it offers a truly unique experience. Rooms start at €200 per night.

Personal Experience: I treated myself to a weekend here. The room was spacious, and the service impeccable. The in-house restaurant is also fantastic, with dinner costing around €50 per person.

Mid-Range: City Hotel Nieuw Minerva at Boommarkt 23 is perfect for those wanting a central location with a moderate budget.

Personal Experience: I stayed here for a week during a business trip. The staff was friendly, and the breakfast buffet was a great way to start the day. Rooms were about €110 per night.

Budget-Friendly: Ibis Leiden Centre at Stationsplein 240-242 is great for budget travelers without sacrificing comfort. Rooms start at €75 per night.

Personal Experience: I stayed here on a quick trip and found it incredibly convenient, especially being right next to the train station.

Conclusion

Choosing the right accommodation in Leiden involves considering a range of factors from your budget and preferences to the location and amenities. By understanding what you need and doing a bit of research, you can find the perfect place to stay that will enhance your overall travel experience.

Leiden is a city rich in history, culture, and beauty, and having a comfortable and convenient place to return to each day makes exploring it all the more enjoyable. Whether you're seeking luxury, a mid-range option, or a budget-friendly stay, there's something for everyone in this charming Dutch city. Safe travels, and enjoy your stay in Leiden!

Chapter 14

Booking Tips and Tricks

Booking a trip to Leiden, Netherlands, can be both exciting and a bit daunting. With so many options available, it's essential to know the best times to book, how to find great deals and discounts, and which booking platforms to use. As someone who has spent considerable time exploring and enjoying Leiden, I have gathered a wealth of personal experiences and insights to help you plan your trip efficiently. Here's a comprehensive guide to ensure you get the most out of your booking experience.

Best Times to Book

One of the first things I learned about booking travel is that timing is everything. Booking your trip at the right time can save you a significant amount of money and stress. Here are some tips from my own experiences:

Advance Booking: Booking your flights and accommodations at least three to six months in advance can often get you the best deals. This is especially true if you plan to visit during peak tourist seasons, such as spring when the tulips are in full bloom, or summer when the weather is perfect for exploring the city. I booked my summer trip to Leiden in March and snagged a great deal on my flight and hotel.

Off-Peak Seasons: If you have the flexibility, consider traveling during the off-peak seasons, such as late autumn or winter. The weather might be cooler, but Leiden's charm remains, and you'll find fewer crowds and lower prices. I visited in November once, and it was delightful to explore the city without the usual hustle and bustle.

Mid-Week Travel: Flying on weekdays, particularly Tuesdays and Wednesdays, can often be cheaper than flying on weekends. This tip has saved me quite a bit on airfare. I once shifted my departure date from a

Friday to a Wednesday and saved nearly $200 on my flight.

Last-Minute Deals: Sometimes, waiting until the last minute can work in your favor, especially if you're flexible with your travel dates and accommodations. I once booked a last-minute weekend trip to Leiden in late September and found a fantastic deal on both my flight and hotel. However, this can be risky during peak seasons, so it's best to have a backup plan.

Finding Deals and Discounts

Scoring deals and discounts can make your trip to Leiden even more enjoyable, knowing you saved money to spend on experiences and dining. Here are some strategies that have worked for me:

Sign Up for Alerts: Websites like Skyscanner and Kayak offer fare alerts that notify you when prices drop for your desired destinations. I signed up for alerts and received notifications for flight deals to

Amsterdam (the closest major airport to Leiden), which helped me book a flight at a great price.

Loyalty Programs: Joining airline and hotel loyalty programs can earn you points and discounts. For example, I'm a member of the KLM Flying Blue program, and I earned enough miles on previous trips to get a significant discount on my flight to Leiden.

Student and Senior Discounts: If you're a student or senior, take advantage of the discounts available to you. When I was a student, I used my International Student Identity Card (ISIC) to get discounts on flights and accommodations. Many museums and attractions in Leiden also offer reduced rates for students and seniors.

Discount Websites: Websites like Groupon often have deals on activities, dining, and even accommodations. Before my trip, I checked Groupon and found a discounted canal cruise in Leiden, which was one of the highlights of my visit.

Bundling: Sometimes, booking a flight and hotel together as a package can save you money. Websites like Expedia and Orbitz offer bundling options. For my first trip to Leiden, I used Expedia to book a flight and hotel package and saved about 15% compared to booking them separately.

Using Booking Platforms

With so many booking platforms available, choosing the right one can make your planning process smoother and more cost-effective. Here are the platforms I've found most useful for booking travel to Leiden:

Skyscanner: This is my go-to platform for comparing flight prices. Skyscanner searches multiple airlines and travel agencies to find the best deals. For my recent trip to Leiden, I found a round-trip flight from New York to Amsterdam for $450 using Skyscanner. Their "Everywhere" feature is also great if you're flexible with your destination and just looking for the best deals.

Booking.com: For accommodations, I rely on Booking.com. It offers a wide range of options, from budget hostels to luxury hotels, and provides detailed reviews from other travelers. I booked a cozy room at Boutique Hotel d'Oude Morsch through Booking.com for $120 per night, and it exceeded my expectations. The site's flexible cancellation policies are also a huge plus.

Airbnb: If you prefer a more local experience, Airbnb is an excellent option. I used Airbnb to book a charming canal-side apartment in the heart of Leiden for $90 per night. Staying in an Airbnb allowed me to live like a local and even cook some of my meals, which was a great way to save money.

Expedia: As mentioned earlier, Expedia is great for booking flight and hotel packages. I've used it several times, and the user interface is easy to navigate. For one of my trips, I booked a flight and hotel package for $850, which included a direct flight and a four-night stay at the Golden Tulip Leiden Centre.

TripAdvisor: For activities and tours, TripAdvisor is incredibly useful. You can read reviews, compare prices, and book directly through the site. I booked a day trip to the Keukenhof Gardens through TripAdvisor for $45, which included transportation and an entry ticket. The reviews and photos helped me choose the best tour.

Trainline: If you're traveling around the Netherlands by train, Trainline is a convenient platform for booking train tickets. I used Trainline to book my train from Amsterdam to Leiden for €11. The site provides schedules, prices, and seat reservations.

Hopper: This app predicts the best times to book flights and accommodations based on historical data. Hopper alerted me when the prices for flights to Amsterdam were likely to drop, and I booked my flight at the optimal time. This saved me around $100 on my airfare.

Personal Tips and Experiences

While using these platforms and strategies, I've learned a few personal tips that can enhance your booking experience and overall trip:

Double-Check Policies: Always read the cancellation and refund policies carefully before booking. During the COVID-19 pandemic, flexible policies became crucial. When I had to change my travel dates, having flexible bookings saved me a lot of stress and money.

Contact Accommodations Directly: Sometimes, contacting the hotel or Airbnb host directly can get you a better rate. For my stay at the Hotel Leiden, I called them at +31 71 573 1731 and mentioned a special offer I saw online. They matched the price and included breakfast, which wasn't originally part of the deal.

Use a Rewards Credit Card: Paying for flights and accommodations with a rewards credit card can earn you points or cashback. I used my Chase Sapphire Preferred card, which offers 2x points on travel expenses. The points I accumulated on my Leiden trip helped fund my next adventure.

Stay Updated: Follow airlines and hotels on social media or sign up for their newsletters. They often announce flash sales and exclusive deals. I follow KLM on Twitter, and once, I snagged a last-minute flight deal they tweeted about.

Check Reviews and Photos: Always read reviews and look at traveler photos before booking accommodations or activities. This can give you a more realistic idea of what to expect. I once avoided booking a hotel that had several negative reviews about cleanliness, thanks to the detailed feedback from other travelers.

Book Directly for Perks: Sometimes, booking directly through a hotel's website can get you extra perks like free breakfast or a room upgrade. When I booked directly through the website of City Hotel Nieuw

Minerva, I received a complimentary breakfast and a canal view room at no extra charge.

My Booking Journey to Leiden

Let me share a personal story about my booking journey to Leiden. For my second trip to this picturesque city, I decided to plan a surprise anniversary getaway for my partner. Here's how I used these tips and platforms to create a memorable trip:

Flight Booking: I started by setting up fare alerts on Skyscanner and Google Flights. After a few weeks, I received an alert about a significant price drop for flights from New York to Amsterdam. I quickly booked the round-trip tickets for $430 each, a fantastic deal for peak travel season in May.

Accommodation: For accommodations, I wanted something special. I browsed through Booking.com and found a lovely boutique hotel called Huys van Leyden, located at Oude Singel 212, 2312 RJ Leiden. The reviews were excellent, and the hotel had a romantic, historic charm that seemed perfect for our anniversary. I booked a deluxe room for $150 per night, and it included a canal view and breakfast.

Activities and Dining: To plan activities, I used TripAdvisor to book a private canal tour, which cost $120 for a two-hour tour. The guide was knowledgeable and made the experience intimate and special. I also reserved a table at Het Prentenkabinet, a highly-rated restaurant located at Kloksteeg 25, 2311 SK Leiden, phone number +31 71 512 0132. The dining experience was exquisite, with a three-course meal costing around €45 per person.

Day Trips: For a day trip, I booked tickets to the Keukenhof Gardens through TripAdvisor for $40 each. This included transportation from Leiden and entry to the gardens. Visiting in May meant we could see the tulips in full bloom, which was a highlight of our trip.

Final Touches: To add a special touch, I arranged for a bouquet of tulips to be waiting in our room upon arrival. I contacted the hotel directly, and they were more than happy to help. This small gesture made the trip even more memorable.

Conclusion: Our anniversary trip to Leiden was magical, and planning it using these booking tips and tricks made everything seamless and enjoyable. From finding the best deals on flights and accommodations to booking unique experiences, every step of the process was made easier with a little knowledge and the right tools.

Planning your trip to Leiden doesn't have to be stressful. With these booking tips and tricks, you'll be well-equipped to find great deals, make informed decisions, and create unforgettable memories in this beautiful Dutch city. Happy travels, and I hope your experience in Leiden is as wonderful as mine!

Chapter 15

Leiden's Culinary Delights

L eiden, a historic city nestled in the heart of the Netherlands, is not only known for its rich academic heritage and picturesque canals but also for its diverse and delectable culinary scene. During my extended stay in this enchanting city, I embarked on a gastronomic adventure that took me from cozy cafés to bustling tapas bars, each offering a unique taste of Leiden's culinary landscape. Join me as I recount my mouthwatering journey through the flavors of Leiden.

Must-Try Dishes

Stroopwafels: A Sweet Dutch Delight

One of the first treats I encountered in Leiden was the stroopwafel. This traditional Dutch delicacy consists of two thin waffle cookies sandwiched together with a layer of sweet, gooey caramel syrup. The best place to enjoy a freshly made stroopwafel is at the Leiden Market, held every Wednesday and Saturday.

Personal Tip: Try to catch the stroopwafel stand early in the day when the waffles are still warm and fresh. A large stroopwafel costs around €2.50.

Haring: A Taste of the Sea

No visit to the Netherlands is complete without trying haring (herring). This raw fish, typically served with onions and pickles, is a staple of Dutch cuisine. I braved my first taste at the Vismarkt (Fish Market) in Leiden, and to my surprise, it was deliciously refreshing.

Personal Tip: Hold the fish by its tail, tilt your head back, and take a bite. It's an experience! A portion of haring typically costs around €3.

Poffertjes: Fluffy Mini Pancakes

Poffertjes are another must-try Dutch treat. These fluffy mini pancakes, often dusted with powdered sugar and served with a knob of butter, are a delightful snack. I found the best poffertjes at Oudt Leyden Pancake House.

Address: Steenstraat 49, 2312 BV Leiden

Phone: +31 71 513 3144

Personal Experience: Sitting by the window, watching people stroll by as I enjoyed a plate of poffertjes (€6.50), was one of my favorite moments in Leiden.

Top Restaurants

In Den Doofpot: A Culinary Masterpiece

One of the most memorable dining experiences I had in Leiden was at In Den Doofpot, a restaurant known for its exquisite cuisine and elegant ambiance. The chef's creative dishes, inspired by both local and international flavors, were a true feast for the senses.

Address: Turfmarkt 9, 2312 CE Leiden

Phone: +31 71 514 4211

Personal Experience: The tasting menu (€65 per person) was a journey through multiple courses, each paired with a perfectly selected wine. The standout dish for me was the venison, cooked to perfection and bursting with flavor.

Puur Eten & Drinken: Farm-to-Table Goodness

Puur Eten & Drinken is a charming restaurant that emphasizes organic and locally sourced ingredients. The menu changes with the seasons, ensuring that every dish is fresh and flavorful.

Address: Nieuwe Rijn 3, 2312 JB Leiden

Phone: +31 71 514 3388

Personal Experience: The atmosphere was cozy and inviting, and the staff were incredibly knowledgeable about the menu. I particularly enjoyed the roasted pumpkin salad (€15), which was both hearty and healthy.

The Bishop: Modern Dutch Cuisine

For a contemporary twist on traditional Dutch dishes, The Bishop is a must-visit. The restaurant combines modern culinary techniques with classic ingredients to create a unique dining experience.

Address: Lange Mare 60, 2312 GS Leiden

Phone: +31 71 512 0061

Personal Experience: The Dutch beef tenderloin (€28) was tender and flavorful, served with seasonal vegetables that complemented the dish perfectly. The chocolate dessert (€8) was the perfect end to a delightful meal.

Cafés and Bakeries

Café Barrera: A Cozy Hideaway

Café Barrera is a cozy spot perfect for a relaxing coffee break or a light lunch. Located in the heart of Leiden, this café offers a wide selection of coffees, teas, and delicious pastries.

Address: Rapenburg 56, 2311 GH Leiden

Phone: +31 71 514 1488

Personal Experience: I often found myself here in the afternoons, sipping on a cappuccino (€3) and indulging in a slice of Dutch apple pie (€4.50). The atmosphere is warm and inviting, making it an ideal place to unwind.

Bakker van Maanen: A Bakery with Tradition

Bakker van Maanen is a traditional Dutch bakery that has been serving Leiden for over a century. Known for its high-quality bread and pastries, this bakery is a local favorite.

Address: Haarlemmerstraat 35, 2312 DM Leiden

Phone: +31 71 512 1313

Personal Experience: Their almond croissant (€2.50) is to die for! I loved stopping by in the mornings to grab a fresh pastry and a cup of coffee before starting my day of exploration.

Roos: Artisanal Coffee and More

Roos is not just a café; it's an experience. This charming spot offers artisanal coffee, homemade cakes, and a variety of sandwiches and salads. The interior is cozy, with a rustic charm that makes you want to linger.

Address: Noordeinde 19, 2311 CA Leiden

Phone: +31 71 512 3173

Personal Experience: The carrot cake (€4) and latte (€3.50) combo became my go-to treat. The friendly staff and relaxed vibe made Roos my favorite spot to spend a lazy afternoon.

Tapas Bars

La Cubanita: A Lively Tapas Experience

La Cubanita is a vibrant tapas bar that brings a taste of Spain to Leiden. With its extensive menu of small plates and lively atmosphere, it's a great place to share a meal with friends.

Address: Beestenmarkt 2, 2312 CC Leiden

Phone: +31 71 514 1544

Personal Experience: The all-you-can-eat tapas (€19.95) was a fantastic deal. I particularly enjoyed the garlic prawns and the patatas bravas. The sangria (€4.50 per glass) was the perfect accompaniment to the meal.

Tabú: Latin Fusion Tapas

Tabú offers a fusion of Latin American flavors in a tapas-style format. The dishes are inspired by the cuisines of Mexico, Peru, and Brazil, providing a unique twist on traditional tapas.

Address: Steenstraat 16, 2312 BS Leiden

Phone: +31 71 514 3394

Personal Experience: The ceviche (€8) and the beef empanadas (€7) were standout dishes. The vibrant décor and upbeat music added to the overall fun and festive atmosphere.

Pipa Streetfood Bar: Eclectic and Delicious

Pipa Streetfood Bar is a relatively new addition to Leiden's culinary scene, offering an eclectic mix of street food-inspired tapas. The menu is diverse, with influences from around the world.

Address: Morsstraat 60, 2312 BM Leiden

Phone: +31 71 514 0404

Personal Experience: The Korean fried chicken (€6) and the halloumi fries (€5) were incredible. I loved the laid-back vibe of the place and the friendly service.

Conclusion

Leiden's culinary scene is as diverse and captivating as its rich history and charming canals. From traditional Dutch treats to international flavors, there's something for every palate. Whether you're indulging in a warm stroopwafel at the market, savoring a gourmet meal at a top restaurant, or sharing tapas with friends at a lively bar, the city offers a wealth of gastronomic delights to explore. My time in Leiden was filled with unforgettable food experiences, and I hope this guid

Chapter 16

Day Trips and Excursions

L eiden is a charming and historic city, but its allure doesn't stop at the city limits. During my time in the Netherlands, I discovered that the surrounding areas offer a wealth of fascinating day trips and excursions. Whether you're into exploring quaint towns, natural wonders, or cultural treasures, there's something for everyone. Here are some of my favorite day trips from Leiden, complete with personal experiences, essential information, and tips.

Nearby Towns and Villages

Delft

One of my most memorable day trips was to Delft, a picturesque town known for its iconic blue and white pottery and its association with the famous painter Johannes Vermeer. Just a 30-minute train ride from Leiden, Delft feels like stepping back in time.

I started my visit at the Royal Delft factory (Rotterdamseweg 196, 2628 AR Delft, phone: +31 15 760 0800). For around €13, you can take a guided tour to see how the beautiful Delftware is made. Watching the artisans at work was mesmerizing, and I couldn't resist buying a small hand-painted tile as a souvenir (€20).

The Vermeer Centrum (Voldergracht 21, 2611 EV Delft, phone: +31 15 213 8588) was another highlight. For €10, you can learn about Vermeer's life and work in the city where he painted most of his masterpieces. The interactive exhibits were particularly engaging, and I left with a much deeper appreciation for his art.

Strolling through Delft's cobbled streets, I couldn't help but be charmed by the Old Church (Oude Kerk) and the New Church (Nieuwe Kerk), where you can climb the tower for a stunning view of the town and beyond. Admission to both churches is €5 each.

For lunch, I recommend De Waag (Markt 11, 2611 GP Delft, phone: +31 15 212 5533), a historic building turned restaurant. The Dutch pancakes here are delicious and cost around €8-€12.

Gouda

Another delightful excursion is to the town of Gouda, famous for its cheese and beautiful stained-glass windows. Gouda is just a 25-minute train ride from Leiden.

I visited on a Thursday morning to catch the Gouda Cheese Market (Markt 35, 2801 JK Gouda, phone: +31 182 588 208), held from April to August. Watching the traditional cheese weighing and bargaining was a unique experience, and sampling the different varieties was a treat. Many stalls offer cheese samples for free, but I bought a small wheel of aged Gouda for €15 to take home.

The St. John's Church (Sint Janskerk, Achter de Kerk 16, 2801 JX Gouda, phone: +31 182 512 684) is a must-see. For €5, you can enter this UNESCO-listed church and marvel at its impressive stained-glass windows, some of the largest in the world.

I had lunch at Kaas en Koffie (Lange Groenendaal 97, 2801 LS Gouda, phone: +31 182 520 045), a cozy café where I enjoyed a cheese platter featuring Gouda cheese in various stages of aging (€12).

Natural Wonders

Keukenhof Gardens

If you're visiting in the spring, a trip to the Keukenhof Gardens (Stationsweg 166A, 2161 AM Lisse, phone: +31 252 465 555) is a must. Located just a 20-minute drive from Leiden, these world-renowned gardens are open from mid-March to mid-May and offer a spectacular display of tulips and other flowers.

I visited in April, and the sight of millions of blooming tulips in every color imaginable was breathtaking. The entrance fee is €19 for adults, but the experience is worth every cent. There are also guided tours available for an additional fee, but I opted to explore the gardens on my own.

For lunch, there are several cafes within the gardens offering light meals and snacks. I enjoyed a traditional Dutch sandwich for €7 while sitting by one of the many scenic ponds.

The Hague's Dunes and Beaches

A short 15-minute train ride from Leiden brought me to The Hague, where I explored the beautiful Meijendel Dunes. This nature reserve offers numerous walking and biking trails through stunning dune landscapes. The visitor center (Meijendelseweg 40, 2243 GN Wassenaar, phone: +31 70 511 2233) provides maps and information about the flora and fauna.

I rented a bike from Fietsverhuur Den Haag (Kerkplein 7, 2513 AZ The Hague, phone: +31 70 201 2630) for €15 a day and spent a leisurely afternoon cycling through the dunes and along the coastline. The fresh sea breeze and the sight of the rolling dunes were incredibly refreshing.

For a relaxing beach experience, I headed to Scheveningen Beach. This bustling seaside area has a long sandy beach, a pier, and plenty of beachfront cafes. I enjoyed a delicious seafood lunch at Simonis aan de Haven (Visafslagweg 20, 2583 DM The Hague, phone: +31 70 350 0022), where I indulged in a seafood platter for €25.

Cultural Excursions

Haarlem

Just a 20-minute train ride from Leiden, Haarlem is a treasure trove of cultural and historical attractions. One of my favorite spots was the Frans Hals Museum (Groot Heiligland 62, 2011 ES Haarlem, phone: +31 23 511 5775). For €16, you can explore the works of this famous Dutch Golden Age painter, housed in a beautiful historic building.

Another highlight was the Teylers Museum (Spaarne 16, 2011 CH Haarlem, phone: +31 23 516 0960), the oldest museum in the Netherlands. The collection of scientific instruments, fossils, and art is fascinating, and the entrance fee is €13.

For lunch, I highly recommend Jopenkerk (Gedempte Voldersgracht 2, 2011 WB Haarlem, phone: +31 23 533 4114), a former church turned brewery and restaurant. Their beer tasting flight (€10) and hearty Dutch dishes (€12-€18) were fantastic.

Zaanse Schans

A bit further afield, about an hour's drive from Leiden, is the Zaanse Schans, an open-air museum showcasing traditional Dutch life. The site features historic windmills, wooden houses, and workshops.

I loved touring the windmills, where you can see how they function and learn about their history. Admission to each windmill is around €5, but a combo ticket for multiple windmills is available for €15.

The Wooden Shoe Workshop (Kraaienest 4, 1509 AZ Zaandam, phone: +31 75 617 7121) was another highlight. Watching the craftsmen make clogs was fascinating, and I couldn't resist buying a small pair of wooden shoes (€20) as a souvenir.

For lunch, I enjoyed a traditional Dutch pancake at De Kraai (Schansend 8, 1509 AW Zaandam, phone: +31 75 616 9145). The pancakes, served with a variety of toppings, cost around €8-€12.

Personal Reflections

Each of these day trips and excursions offered a unique glimpse into the diverse beauty and culture of the Netherlands. From the bustling cheese markets of Gouda to the serene dunes of The Hague, every experience enriched my understanding and appreciation of this charming country.

One of the most memorable moments was during my visit to Keukenhof Gardens. As I wandered through the vibrant tulip fields, I struck up a conversation with a local gardener who shared stories of the garden's history and the meticulous care that goes into maintaining the flowers. This interaction made my visit even more special and reminded me of the importance of connecting with locals during travel.

In Haarlem, I had the pleasure of meeting a friendly shop owner who recommended some lesser-known sights and shared fascinating anecdotes about the town's history. These personal interactions added a layer of depth to my travels that no guidebook could provide.

Exploring the windmills at Zaanse Schans was another highlight. Climbing to the top of a windmill and looking out over the scenic landscape was a surreal experience. It felt like stepping back in time, and I was grateful for the opportunity to witness such a well-preserved piece of Dutch heritage.

In conclusion, day trips and excursions from Leiden offer a perfect blend of history, culture, and natural beauty. Whether you're exploring quaint towns, marveling at natural wonders, or immersing yourself in cultural experiences, each adventure promises to leave you with cherished memories and a deeper appreciation for the Netherlands. So, pack your bags, embrace the spirit of adventure, and let Leiden be your gateway to these incredible destinations. Happy travels!

Chapter 17

When to Visit Leiden

Leiden, a charming university city in the Netherlands, holds a special place in my heart. This historic city, with its picturesque canals, lush parks, and vibrant culture, offers a perfect blend of tranquility and excitement. Having spent a considerable amount of time here, I've experienced Leiden through its many seasons and events. Here's my comprehensive guide on when to visit this beautiful city, highlighting the best seasons, key events, and off-peak travel tips.

Best Seasons and Weather

Spring: A Blooming Marvel

Spring in Leiden is a sight to behold. As the city shakes off the chill of winter, it bursts into life with vibrant colors. Tulips, daffodils, and hyacinths bloom in every corner, making it a perfect time to visit the Keukenhof Gardens, just a short drive away.

Weather: Temperatures range from 8°C (46°F) in March to 17°C (63°F) in May. Expect occasional rain showers.

Personal Experience: I remember my first spring in Leiden vividly. Walking along the canals lined with blooming flowers felt like stepping into a painting. The annual Bloemencorso Bollenstreek (Flower Parade) in April was a highlight, with elaborate floral floats passing through the city.

Summer: Vibrant and Lively

Summer is peak tourist season in Leiden, and for good reason. The weather is warm, and the city is buzzing with activity. Outdoor terraces are packed with people enjoying drinks, and the canals are filled with boats.

Weather: Average temperatures range from 18°C (64°F) in June to 22°C (72°F) in August. It's the sunniest time of the year, though rain showers can still occur.

Personal Experience: One summer, I rented a bike and explored the countryside around Leiden. Cycling past windmills and lush green fields under the clear blue sky was an unforgettable experience. The Leiden Lakenfeesten (Leiden Cloth Festival) in June, with its boat parade and concerts, was another summer highlight.

Autumn: A Golden Retreat

Autumn in Leiden is serene and beautiful. The foliage transforms into shades of gold and red, and the city takes on a quieter, more introspective vibe.

Weather: Temperatures drop from 17°C (63°F) in September to 9°C (48°F) in November. Rain becomes more frequent.

Personal Experience: Autumn walks along the tree-lined canals were a favorite pastime of mine. The crisp air and the rustling leaves created a magical atmosphere. I also enjoyed the 3 October Festival, celebrating the Relief of Leiden, with its lively parades and traditional herring and white bread.

Winter: Cozy and Festive

Winter in Leiden can be cold, but it has its own charm. The city is adorned with festive lights, and the canals sometimes freeze, creating a picturesque winter wonderland.

Weather: Temperatures range from 6°C (43°F) in December to 3°C (37°F) in February. Snow is rare but possible.

Personal Experience: I spent one winter holiday season in Leiden, and it was enchanting. The Leiden Winter Wonder Week in December, with its ice rink and Christmas market, was delightful. I also loved visiting the Museum De Lakenhal, which provided a warm escape from the chilly weather.

Key Events and Festivals

Bloemencorso Bollenstreek (Flower Parade)

Held in April, the Bloemencorso Bollenstreek is a spectacular event showcasing the beauty of Dutch flowers. Elaborate floats decorated with tulips, daffodils, and hyacinths parade through the streets of Leiden.

Personal Tip: Arrive early to secure a good viewing spot. Bring a camera to capture the stunning floral displays.

Leiden Lakenfeesten (Leiden Cloth Festival)

This festival, held in June, celebrates Leiden's historical cloth industry. The city comes alive with boat parades, concerts, and various family-friendly activities.

Personal Tip: Don't miss the Dragon Boat Race on the Nieuwe Rijn. It's a thrilling event with teams paddling fiercely to the finish line.

3 October Festival

The 3 October Festival commemorates the Relief of Leiden in 1574, when the city was liberated from Spanish siege. The celebrations include parades, concerts, and traditional foods like herring and white bread.

Personal Tip: Visit the funfair at the Beestenmarkt and enjoy the lively atmosphere. It's a great way to experience Dutch culture and history.

Leiden Winter Wonder Week

In December, Leiden transforms into a winter wonderland. The Leiden Winter Wonder Week features an ice rink, Christmas market, and festive decorations throughout the city.

Personal Tip: Warm up with a cup of hot chocolate or Glühwein from one of the market stalls. The ice rink at the Nieuwe Rijn is a fun activity for all ages.

Off-Peak Travel Tips

Exploring Leiden Without the Crowds

Traveling during off-peak seasons has its advantages. Here are some tips for making the most of your visit when the city is less crowded.

Visit in Early Spring or Late Autumn: These shoulder seasons offer mild weather and fewer tourists. You'll have more space to explore attractions and enjoy a more relaxed atmosphere.

Stay in Local Accommodations: Consider staying in a bed and breakfast or a local guesthouse. They often provide a more authentic experience and personalized service. One of my favorites is Huys van Leyden, located at Oude Singel 212, with rooms starting at around €100 per night. Phone: +31 71 260 0016.

Enjoy Indoor Attractions: Leiden has several excellent museums and cultural sites that are perfect for off-peak visits. The Rijksmuseum van Oudheden (National Museum of Antiquities) and the Naturalis Biodiversity Center are both fascinating and less crowded during these times.

Try Local Cuisine: With fewer tourists, you'll have an easier time getting reservations at popular restaurants. I recommend Restaurant In Den Doofpot, located at Turfmarkt 9, for a fine dining experience with a meal costing around €40-€60 per person. Phone: +31 71 512 2434.

Seasonal Activities

Each season in Leiden offers unique activities that can enhance your travel experience. Here are some suggestions based on my own adventures:

Spring: Visit the Keukenhof Gardens to see the stunning tulip displays. The gardens are open from mid-March to mid-May. Tickets cost around €19 for adults.

Summer: Rent a boat and cruise the canals. Several companies offer boat rentals, such as Greenjoy, located at Zijlstroom 2. Prices start at around €40 per hour. Phone: +31 85 401 4545.

Autumn: Take a scenic bike ride through the surrounding countryside. The Vlietland recreational area is perfect for cycling and is just a short ride from the city center.

Winter: Enjoy the festive atmosphere at the Christmas market and ice rink. The market is located at Nieuwe Rijn and runs from mid-December to early January. Entry to the market is free, and ice skating costs around €7 per person.

Practical Tips

Weather Preparedness: The Netherlands is known for its unpredictable weather. Always carry an umbrella and wear layers, especially during spring and autumn.

Transportation: Leiden is well-connected by public transport. The Leiden Central Station is the main hub, with frequent trains to Amsterdam, The Hague, and other major cities. Buses and bikes are also great ways to get around locally.

Language: While Dutch is the official language, most people in Leiden speak English. Learning a few basic Dutch phrases, however, can enhance your experience and interactions with locals.

Currency: The currency in the Netherlands is the Euro (€). Credit cards are widely accepted, but it's a good idea to carry some cash for small purchases.

Conclusion

Leiden is a city that can be enjoyed year-round, each season offering its own unique charm and activities. Whether you're marveling at the spring blooms, soaking up the summer sun, savoring the autumn colors, or embracing the winter festivities, Leiden promises an unforgettable experience. The key events and festivals add vibrant cultural experiences, while off-peak travel allows for a more relaxed and intimate exploration of the city's beauty.

Having lived through each season in Leiden, I can attest to the city's timeless appeal and the warmth of its people. Whenever you choose to visit, Leiden will welcome you with open arms and a wealth of memories waiting to be made. Safe travels and enjoy every moment in this enchanting Dutch gem!

Chapter 18

Health and Safety in Leiden

When traveling to a new destination, especially one as charming and historically rich as Leiden, it's essential to prioritize your health and safety. During my unforgettable time in Leiden, I made sure to familiarize myself with various health tips, safety precautions, and emergency contacts to ensure a smooth and worry-free trip. Here's a comprehensive guide based on my experiences.

Essential Health Tips

Staying Healthy While Traveling

Traveling can sometimes take a toll on your health, especially if you're not prepared. Here are some tips I found particularly useful:

Stay Hydrated: Drinking plenty of water is crucial, especially if you're exploring the city on foot or by bike. Tap water in Leiden is safe to drink, so carry a reusable water bottle with you. I purchased mine from Dille & Kamille, a delightful store located at Nieuwe Rijn 2, 2312 JC Leiden. Their phone number is +31 71 512 5533.

Eat Balanced Meals: Dutch cuisine is delicious but can be quite rich. Make sure to balance your diet with fresh fruits and vegetables. Markets like the Leiden Saturday Market, held at Nieuwe Rijn and Vismarkt, offer a variety of fresh produce. This market is a feast for the senses, with vibrant stalls and friendly vendors.

Rest Well: After a day of exploring, getting a good night's sleep is essential. I stayed at the Boutique Hotel d'Oude Morsch, located at Park de Put 1, 2312 BM Leiden. Their phone number is +31 71 531 0622. The rooms are comfortable, and the ambiance is perfect for relaxing after a busy day.

Carry a Basic First Aid Kit: It's always a good idea to have a small first aid kit with you. Mine included band-aids, antiseptic wipes, pain relievers, and any personal medications. You can purchase these items from local pharmacies such as BENU Apotheek, found at Haarlemmerstraat 178, 2312 GE Leiden. Their phone number is +31 71 514 1112.

Stay Active: Leiden is a very walkable city, and biking is a popular mode of transport. Renting a bike from EasyFiets, located at Haagweg 8, 2311 AA Leiden (phone number: +31 71 512 9789), was one of the best decisions I made. It allowed me to explore the city actively and enjoy the beautiful canals and historic streets.

Staying Safe

General Safety Tips

Leiden is a relatively safe city, but it's always good to take standard precautions to ensure your well-being:

Be Aware of Your Surroundings: Whether you're walking through the bustling city center or the quieter residential areas, always stay alert. Keep your belongings secure and avoid flashing valuables.

Use Reliable Transportation: If you're traveling late at night, it's best to use trusted taxi services. I found Taxi Centrale Leiden to be reliable. They can be reached at +31 71 210 0210.

Know the Local Emergency Number: The general emergency number in the Netherlands is 112. This number connects you to police, fire, and medical emergency services.

Secure Your Accommodation: Ensure that your hotel or rental accommodation has good security measures. When I stayed at City Hotel Rembrandt, located at Nieuwe Beestenmarkt 10, 2312 CH Leiden (phone number: +31 71 512 0210), I was impressed by their secure entry system and attentive staff.

Stay Informed: Keep an eye on local news and updates. I found it useful to follow local news websites and social media channels for any important announcements or safety alerts.

Specific Safety Concerns

Biking Safety: Biking is very common in Leiden, but make sure to follow local biking rules. Always use bike lanes, signal your turns, and be mindful of pedestrians. Wearing a helmet, although not mandatory, is advisable for safety.

Night Safety: While Leiden is generally safe at night, it's wise to stick to well-lit and populated areas if you're out late. Avoid walking alone in secluded areas.

Weather Preparedness: The weather in Leiden can be unpredictable. Always check the weather forecast before heading out and dress accordingly. In winter, roads and sidewalks can be slippery, so wear appropriate footwear.

Having a list of emergency contacts is crucial for any traveler. Here are some important numbers and addresses I noted during my stay:

Police, Fire, and Medical Emergencies: Dial 112 for immediate assistance.

Non-Emergency Medical Help: For non-urgent medical issues, you can visit the local hospital, Alrijne Hospital Leiden, located at Houtlaan 55, 2334 CK Leiden. Their phone number is +31 71 517 8178.

Pharmacies: If you need to fill a prescription or get over-the-counter medication, BENU Apotheek (Haarlemmerstraat 178, 2312 GE Leiden, phone: +31 71 514 1112) is a reliable option.

Dental Emergencies: For dental issues, Tandartspraktijk M.H.C. Wouters, located at Oude

Vest 45, 2312 XS Leiden, offers emergency dental services. Their phone number is +31 71 514 1877.

Embassies and Consulates: If you lose your passport or need consular assistance, contact your country's embassy or consulate in the Netherlands. Most embassies are located in The Hague, a short train ride from Leiden.

Tourist Information: The VVV Leiden Tourist Information Center is very helpful for tourists needing assistance. They are located at Stationsweg 26, 2312 AV Leiden, and can be reached at +31 71 516 6000.

Lost and Found: If you lose something, check with the local police station or contact Leiden's Lost and Found office. The main police station is located at Langegracht 11, 2312 NV Leiden, phone number +31 900 8844.

Personal Experiences and Tips

During my time in Leiden, I had a couple of experiences that taught me valuable lessons about health and safety. One evening, I decided to explore the city on foot and ended up losing my way in a less populated area. Thankfully, I had the emergency number saved on my phone and was able to call a taxi to take me back to my hotel. This experience underscored the importance of staying within familiar or well-populated areas, especially after dark.

Another memorable incident involved a minor bike accident. I was cycling through one of the narrow streets when I collided with another cyclist. We were both fine, but it reminded me of the importance of wearing a helmet and being extra cautious, especially in busy areas. I visited the nearby Alrijne Hospital for a quick check-up, and the staff there were incredibly kind and efficient.

I also found it helpful to carry a small travel insurance card with me. My travel insurance covered medical expenses, and having the card handy made the process at the hospital smoother. If you don't already have travel insurance, I highly recommend getting it before your trip. It's a small expense compared to the peace of mind it provides.

In conclusion, while Leiden is a beautiful and relatively safe city, taking these health and safety precautions can make your visit even more enjoyable. From staying hydrated and eating well to knowing emergency contacts and biking safely, these tips will help ensure you have a wonderful and worry-free time in this historic Dutch city. Safe travels, and enjoy every moment of your stay in Leiden!

Chapter 19

Language Tips for Travelers in Leiden, Netherlands

L eiden! A city that effortlessly marries the charm of its historical significance with the lively energy of a university town. Nestled in the province of South Holland, Leiden is famous for its picturesque canals, stunning architecture, and rich cultural heritage. During my time in this beautiful city, I realized that while many locals speak English, knowing a bit of Dutch can greatly enhance your experience. In this chapter, I'll share some useful language tips that I found invaluable during my stay, peppered with personal anecdotes and practical advice.

Basic Phrases

Greetings and Essentials

Learning a few basic Dutch phrases can go a long way in making your interactions more pleasant and meaningful. Here are some fundamental phrases that I found particularly useful:

Hello / Hi: Hallo / Hoi

Good morning: Goedemorgen

Good afternoon: Goedemiddag

Good evening: Goedenavond

Goodbye: Tot ziens

Please: Alsjeblieft (informal) / Alstublieft (formal)

Thank you: Dank je (informal) / Dank u (formal)

Yes / No: Ja / Nee

Excuse me / Sorry: Pardon / Sorry

Personal Experience: On my first day, I visited a charming café called Het Leidse Huys (Address: Breestraat 161, Leiden | Phone: +31 71 514 1010). I greeted the barista with a cheerful "Goedemorgen!" and her face lit up with a smile. It was a small gesture, but it made my coffee run feel a bit more special.

Common Questions

Interacting with locals often involves asking questions. Here are some common queries and how to phrase them:

Where is...? Waar is...?

How much does it cost? Hoeveel kost het?

Do you speak English? Spreekt u Engels?

What time is it? Hoe laat is het?

Can you help me? Kunt u mij helpen?

Personal Tip: When I was at the Museum De Lakenhal (Address: Oude Singel 32, Leiden | Phone: +31 71 516 5360), I needed directions to the exhibition hall. I approached a staff member and asked, "Waar is de tentoonstellingshal?" It was gratifying to see how my effort to speak Dutch was appreciated, and it made the interaction smoother.

Helpful Expressions

Dining Out

Leiden has a fantastic culinary scene, and knowing some restaurant-specific phrases can enhance your dining experience:

I would like to order... Ik zou graag ... willen bestellen.

The bill, please. De rekening, alstublieft.

A table for two, please. Een tafel voor twee, alstublieft.

Do you have a vegetarian option? Heeft u een vegetarische optie?

Personal Experience: At Restaurant In Den Doofpot (Address: Turfmarkt 9, Leiden | Phone: +31 71 513 8000), I asked, "Heeft u een vegetarische optie?" The waiter was happy to point out the vegetarian dishes, and I enjoyed a delightful meal knowing exactly what I was eating.

Shopping

Whether you're browsing local markets or shopping for souvenirs, these phrases will come in handy:

How much is this? Hoeveel kost dit?

Can I try this on? Kan ik dit passen?

Do you accept credit cards? Accepteert u creditcards?

I'm just looking. Ik kijk alleen even.

Personal Tip: At the bustling Saturday Market on Nieuwe Rijn, I wanted to buy some traditional Dutch cheese. I asked the vendor, "Hoeveel kost dit?" and then sampled a few varieties before making my purchase. It made the shopping experience much more engaging.

Language Resources

Books and Apps

For those looking to delve deeper into Dutch, there are plenty of resources available:

Books: "Dutch for Dummies" is a great starting point. It's comprehensive and easy to follow.

Apps: Duolingo and Babbel are excellent for learning on the go. They offer interactive lessons that are both fun and educational.

Phrasebooks: Lonely Planet's Dutch Phrasebook & Dictionary is handy for quick references.

Personal Experience: I used the Duolingo app extensively during my stay. Every morning, I would practice a few lessons before heading out. This routine not only improved my Dutch but also boosted my confidence when speaking to locals.

Local Classes

If you're planning an extended stay in Leiden, consider enrolling in a local language class. The Universiteit Leiden's Academic Language Centre (Address: Pieter de la Courtgebouw, Wassenaarseweg 52, Leiden | Phone: +31 71 527 2332) offers Dutch courses for non-native speakers. These classes are a fantastic way to learn the language in a structured environment.

Personal Tip: I took a short course at the Academic Language Centre, and it was immensely helpful. The instructors were patient and knowledgeable, and I met several other expats, which added a social dimension to my learning experience.

Language Exchange

Language exchange meetups are a fun way to practice Dutch and make new friends. Websites like Meetup.com often list language exchange events in Leiden. Cafés like Stadscafé Van der Werff (Address: Steenstraat 2, Leiden | Phone: +31 71 514 7207) host regular language exchange evenings where you can practice Dutch with locals and fellow travelers.

Personal Experience: I attended a language exchange event at Stadscafé Van der Werff, and it was a highlight of my trip. Over beers and bitterballen, I practiced Dutch with native speakers and shared stories with people from all over the world.

Conclusion

Leiden's rich history, beautiful canals, and vibrant cultural scene make it a fantastic destination for travelers. While many locals speak English, making an effort to learn some Dutch phrases can greatly enhance your experience. Not only does it show respect for the local culture, but it also opens up more meaningful interactions with the people you meet.

From greeting the friendly barista at Het Leidse Huys to asking for directions at the Museum De Lakenhal, my attempts at speaking Dutch were always met with appreciation. Whether dining at Restaurant In Den Doofpot or shopping at the Saturday Market on Nieuwe Rijn, knowing a bit of the local language made my experiences richer and more rewarding.

Leiden is a city that invites you to explore, learn, and connect. Embrace the language, dive into the culture, and you'll find that your time here is filled with unforgettable moments and cherished memories. Tot ziens, en veel plezier in Leiden! (Goodbye, and have fun in Leiden!)

Chapter 20

Sustainable and Responsible Tourism in Leiden

When I first arrived in Leiden, Netherlands, I was immediately taken by the city's charm. Its historic canals, cobblestone streets, and vibrant culture were everything I had hoped for. But as a responsible traveler, I also wanted to ensure that my visit left a positive impact on this beautiful city. Here's a guide based on my experiences on how you can practice sustainable and responsible tourism in Leiden.

Eco-Friendly Practices

Reducing Waste

One of the easiest ways to be eco-friendly is by reducing waste. During my stay, I always carried a reusable water bottle. The tap water in Leiden is clean and safe to drink, which made it easy to refill my bottle and avoid buying plastic water bottles. I bought my reusable bottle at a local store called Dille & Kamille, located at Nieuwe Rijn 11, 2312 JC Leiden. Their phone number is +31 71 512 4287.

I also made sure to bring a reusable shopping bag. This came in handy when shopping at the local markets. For instance, at the bustling Saturday market on Nieuwe Rijn, I bought fresh produce, cheese, and other local goods, all without using plastic bags. It's a small step, but it makes a big difference.

Using Public Transportation and Biking

Leiden is a compact city, and its public transportation system is excellent. I frequently used buses and trams, which are both efficient and eco-friendly. The main bus station, Leiden Centraal, is located at Stationsplein, 2312 AJ Leiden. You can contact them at +31 900 9292 for schedules and routes.

Biking is another fantastic way to get around. The city is incredibly bike-friendly, with dedicated bike lanes and parking everywhere. I rented a bike from EasyFiets, a bike rental shop located at Langegracht 4, 2312 NV Leiden. Their phone number is +31 71 514 0918, and they offer affordable rates starting at €10 per day. Cycling not only reduces your carbon footprint but also allows you to explore the city at your own pace.

Staying at Eco-Friendly Accommodations

Choosing eco-friendly accommodations was a priority for me. I stayed at Boutique Hotel d'Oude Morsch, which is known for its sustainability efforts. The hotel uses energy-efficient systems, recycles waste, and promotes water conservation. It's located at Park de Put 1, 2312 BM Leiden, and you can reach them at +31 71 260 1260. The rooms are comfortable, the staff is friendly, and knowing that I was supporting an eco-conscious business made my stay even more enjoyable.

Another great option is Steenhof Suites, located at Steenstraat 1, 2312 BS Leiden. Their phone number is +31 71 514 7303. They also emphasize sustainability and offer a cozy, luxurious stay.

Eating Locally and Sustainably

Food is a significant part of any travel experience, and in Leiden, I made it a point to eat at local, sustainable restaurants. One of my favorites was Het Prentenkabinet, located at Kloksteeg 25, 2311 SK Leiden. Their phone number is +31 71 512 1780. They focus on locally sourced ingredients, and their seasonal menu is a delight. Dining there not only supports local farmers but also reduces the carbon footprint associated with transporting food.

Another excellent spot is Restaurant In den Doofpot, situated at Turfmarkt 9, 2312 CE Leiden. Their phone number is +31 71 512 2434. They offer a fantastic farm-to-table dining experience, with dishes that highlight regional specialties.

Supporting Local Communities

Shopping at Local Markets and Shops

Supporting local businesses is crucial for sustainable tourism. The Saturday market at Nieuwe Rijn is a must-visit. It's a vibrant place where you can find everything from fresh produce to handmade crafts. I spent many Saturdays browsing the stalls, chatting with vendors, and buying unique souvenirs. It's open from 8 AM to 5 PM, and the atmosphere is always lively and welcoming.

For unique gifts and souvenirs, I recommend visiting De Bonte Koe, a delightful chocolate shop at Nieuwe Rijn 18, 2312 JC Leiden. Their phone number is +31 71 514 8235. The chocolates are made on-site, and the flavors are incredible. Buying from local artisans ensures your money supports the community directly.

Dining at Family-Owned Restaurants

One of the best ways to support local communities is by dining at family-owned restaurants. Pannenkoekenhuis de Schaapsbel, located at Beestenmarkt 4, 2312 CC Leiden, is a charming pancake house. Their phone number is +31 71 513 4901. The pancakes are delicious, and the warm, friendly atmosphere makes it a great place to enjoy a meal.

Another gem is Restaurant De Gaanderij, located at Nieuwe Rijn 27, 2312 JE Leiden. You can contact them at +31 71 513 2223. This family-run restaurant offers traditional Dutch cuisine with a modern twist. The owners are passionate about their food and their city, and it shows in every dish they serve.

Participating in Community Activities

Engaging in community activities is a rewarding way to support locals. During my stay, I joined a walking tour organized by the Leiden Tourist Information Office. The guides were locals who shared fascinating stories about the city's history and culture. The office is located at Stationsweg 26, 2312 AV Leiden, and their phone number is +31 71 516 6000.

I also participated in a canal cleanup event organized by Plastic Spotter, a local initiative aimed at reducing plastic pollution in Leiden's canals. It was a great way to meet locals, learn about their environmental efforts, and contribute to a cleaner city. You can find out more about their activities by contacting them at +31 6 1225 8885.

Minimizing Your Footprint

Conserving Energy and Water

Small actions can significantly reduce your environmental footprint. In my hotel, I made sure to turn off lights, air conditioning, and electronic devices when not in use. I also reused towels and linens, which many hotels encourage as part of their sustainability programs.

Conserving water is equally important. I took shorter showers and avoided letting the water run unnecessarily. In a city that values its natural resources, these small efforts can make a big difference.

Reducing Plastic Use

Reducing plastic use was a priority during my stay in Leiden. I avoided single-use plastics by carrying reusable utensils and straws. When shopping, I opted for products with minimal or eco-friendly packaging. Many local shops, like Marqt at Nieuwe Rijn 51, 2312 JG Leiden (phone: +31 71 514 7586), offer biodegradable bags or encourage you to bring your own.

Respecting Local Wildlife and Nature

Leiden is home to beautiful parks and natural reserves. One of my favorite spots was Hortus botanicus, located at Rapenburg 73, 2311 GJ Leiden. Their phone number is +31 71 527 7249. This botanical garden is a peaceful oasis in the city. When visiting such places, it's essential to stay on designated paths, avoid picking plants, and refrain from disturbing wildlife.

Another highlight was a visit to the Kagerplassen, a stunning area of lakes and wetlands perfect for boating and bird watching. You can rent a boat from Olympia Charters, located at Zijldijk 28, 2352 AB Leiderdorp. Their phone number is +31 71 589 3010.

Remember to respect the natural habitat and leave no trace of your visit.

Educating Yourself and Others

Understanding the impact of your actions and educating others about responsible tourism can amplify your efforts. During my time in Leiden, I took the opportunity to learn about the city's sustainability initiatives. For instance, the University of Leiden has numerous programs and research projects focused on environmental conservation and sustainability. You can visit their sustainability office at Rapenburg 70, 2311 EZ Leiden, or contact them at +31 71 527 2727 for more information.

Sharing what you learn with fellow travelers can help spread awareness and encourage more people to adopt sustainable practices. Every small action counts, and together we can make a significant impact.

Personal Reflections

Reflecting on my time in Leiden, I'm grateful for the opportunity to explore this incredible city while practicing sustainable and responsible tourism. The connections I made with locals, the beautiful sights I saw, and the knowledge I gained about environmental stewardship have enriched my travel experience in ways I hadn't imagined.

One of my most cherished memories was a quiet afternoon spent at the Burcht van Leiden, an ancient fortification offering panoramic views of the city. Sitting there, surrounded by history and nature, I felt a deep sense of responsibility to preserve the beauty of such places for future generations.

Another highlight was attending the Leiden International Film Festival. This event not only showcased fantastic films but also promoted sustainability by minimizing waste and using eco-friendly materials. The festival is held annually in November, and I highly recommend checking it out if you're in town. You can contact the festival organizers at +31 71 516 6000 for more details.

Traveling sustainably isn't just about making eco-friendly choices; it's about connecting with the places you visit on a deeper level. It's about understanding the impact of your actions and making conscious decisions that benefit the environment and local communities. Leiden, with its rich history, vibrant culture, and commitment to sustainability, is a perfect place to practice responsible tourism.

As you plan your visit to Leiden, I encourage you to consider these practices and make your journey as meaningful and impactful as possible. The joy of travel lies not just in seeing new places but in ensuring that those places remain beautiful and vibrant for generations to come. Happy travels, and may your time in Leiden be as wonderful and fulfilling as mine was!

Useful Contacts

Having a list of important contacts at your fingertips can make your trip to Leiden smoother and more enjoyable. Here are some key numbers and addresses you might need:

Emergency Services

Police: 112

Ambulance: 112

Fire Department: 112

Hospitals

Leiden University Medical Center (LUMC): Albinusdreef 2, 2333 ZA Leiden | Phone: +31 71 526 9111

Tourist Information

VVV Leiden (Tourist Information Office): Stationsweg 26, 2312 AV Leiden | Phone: +31 71 516 6000

Transportation

Leiden Central Station: Stationsplein 1, 2312 AJ Leiden | Phone: +31 30 235 7822 (NS Customer Service)

Airport

Amsterdam Schiphol Airport: Evert van de Beekstraat 202, 1118 CP Schiphol | Phone: +31 20 794 0800

Maps & Navigation

Navigating Leiden is a delightful experience with its compact size and well-marked streets. Here's where you can find maps and navigation tools:

Printed Maps: Available at the VVV Leiden (Tourist Information Office).

Digital Maps: Google Maps and Maps.me are great options for navigating the city on your smartphone.

Map of Leiden

https://maps.app.goo.gl/xYgQC1tNHf33sYrW8

SCAN THE
IMAGE/QR CODE
WITH YOUR PHONE
TO GET THE
LOCATIONS IN
REAL TIME.

Map of Things to do in Leiden

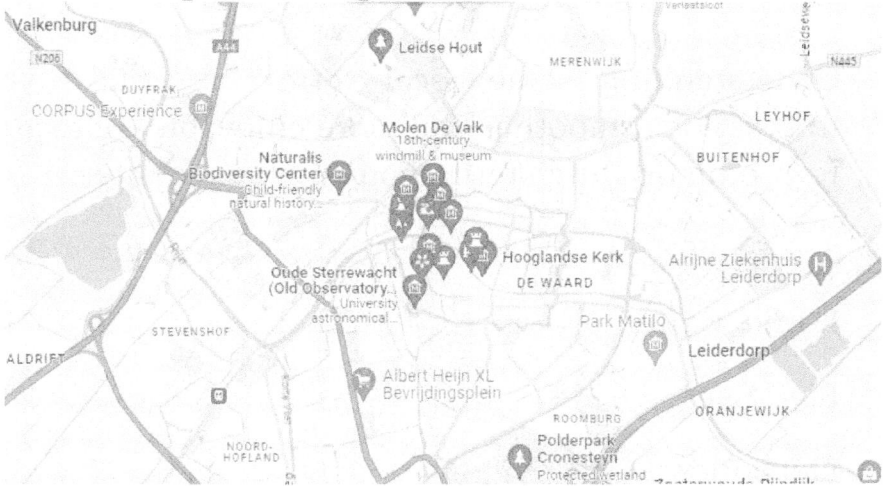

https://www.google.com/maps/search/things+to+do+in++Leiden+/@52.1581554,4.4447687,13z/data=!3m1!4b1?entry=ttu

SCAN THE
IMAGE/QR CODE
WITH YOUR
PHONE TO GET
THE LOCATIONS
IN REAL TIME.

Glossary: Local Terms

Understanding some local terms can make your interactions smoother and more enjoyable. Here are a few common Dutch terms you might encounter:

Koffie: Coffee

Bier: Beer

Fiets: Bicycle

Gracht: Canal

Markt: Market

Straat: Street

Plein: Square

Applications and Useful Resources

These apps and resources can enhance your travel experience in Leiden:

Google Maps: For navigation and finding places from your current location.

Duolingo: To learn basic Dutch phrases.

NS Reisplanner: For train schedules and planning.

TripAdvisor: For reviews and recommendations on attractions, restaurants, and accommodations.

Uber: For easy transportation around the city.

Addresses and Locations of Popular Accommodations

Hotels

1. Boutique Hotel d'Oude Morsch:

Address: Park de Put 1, 2312 BM Leiden

Phone: +31 71 260 0009

2. Van der Valk Hotel Leiden:

Address: Haagse Schouwweg 14, 2332 KG Leiden

Phone: +31 71 573 1731

3. Rembrandt Hotel Leiden:

Address: Nieuwe Beestenmarkt 10, 2312 CH Leiden

Phone: +31 71 566 0551

Addresses and Locations of Popular Restaurants and Cafés

Restaurants

1. Oudt Leyden:

Address: Steenstraat 49, 2312 BS Leiden

Phone: +31 71 512 2444

2. Puur Eten & Drinken:

Address: Botermarkt 21, 2311 EM Leiden

Phone: +31 71 514 2332

3. The Bishop:

Address: Rembrandtstraat 9, 2311 VW Leiden

Phone: +31 71 514 3388

Cafés

1. Café Barrera:

Address: Rapenburg 56, 2311 GH Leiden

Phone: +31 71 512 4009

2. Het Leidse Huys:

Address: Breestraat 161, 2311 CL Leiden

Phone: +31 71 514 1010

3. Lot & de Walvis:

Address: Haven 1, 2312 MG Leiden

Phone: +31 71 514 1250

Addresses and Locations of Popular Bars and Clubs

Bars

1. Café Einstein:

Address: Nieuwe Rijn 19, 2312 JC Leiden

Phone: +31 71 514 7766

2. Olivier Grand Café:

Address: Hooigracht 23, 2312 KM Leiden

Phone: +31 71 576 1244

3. Bar Lokaal:

Address: Hartesteeg 13, 2312 JW Leiden

Phone: +31 71 889 4462

Clubs

1. InCasa:

Address: Lammermarkt 100, 2312 CW Leiden

Phone: +31 71 512 1010

2. Next:

Address: Steenstraat 123, 2312 BV Leiden

Phone: +31 71 514 4300

Addresses and Locations of Top Attractions

Museums and Historical Sites

1. Rijksmuseum van Oudheden (National Museum of Antiquities):

Address: Rapenburg 28, 2311 EW Leiden

Phone: +31 71 516 3163

2. Naturalis Biodiversity Center:

Address: Darwinweg 2, 2333 CR Leiden

Phone: +31 71 751 9519

3. Museum De Lakenhal:

Address: Oude Singel 32, 2312 RA Leiden

Phone: +31 71 516 5360

Parks and Gardens

1. Hortus Botanicus Leiden:

Address: Rapenburg 73, 2311 GJ Leiden

Phone: +31 71 527 7249

2. Van der Werfpark:

Address: 2312 VR Leiden (No phone number available)

Cultural Venues

1. Stadsgehoorzaal Leiden:

Address: Breestraat 60, 2311 CS Leiden

Phone: +31 71 516 3880

2. Leiden University Observatory:

Address: Sterrewachtlaan 11, 2311 GP Leiden

Phone: +31 71 527 5733

With this appendix, you are well-prepared to explore and enjoy all that Leiden has to offer. From essential contacts to top attractions, this guide ensures that you have all the information you need at your fingertips. Enjoy your journey in this beautiful and historic city!

Photo Attribute/Images

https://commons.wikimedia.org/wiki/File:Schiphol-plaza-ns.jpg

https://www.freepik.com/free-photo/beautiful-tropical-beach-sea-with-coconut-palm-tree-paradise-island_3661769.htm#fromView=search&page=9&position=42&uuid=d6136939-942b-4463-a067-7832bedf74dc

https://www.freepik.com/search?format=search&last_filter=page&last_value=5&page=5&query=Leeuwarden#uuid=d6136939-942b-4463-a067-7832bedf74dc

SCAN TO SEE ALL BOOKS TO DIFFERENT
CITIES IN THE NETHERLANDS

Made in the USA
Coppell, TX
20 February 2025

46197125R00125